THE PIG WAR
AND THE
PELICAN GIRLS

THE PIG WAR
AND THE
PELICAN GIRLS

21 EXTRAORDINARY *and* FORGOTTEN STORIES *from* AMERICAN HISTORY

JOE CUHAJ

Prometheus Books

Essex, Connecticut

⊞ Prometheus Books
An imprint of The Globe Pequot Publishing Group, Inc.
64 South Main St.
Essex, CT 06426
www.prometheusbooks.com

Distributed by NATIONAL BOOK NETWORK

British Library Cataloguing in Publication Information Available

Library of Congress Cataloging-in-Publication Data

Names: Cuhaj, Joe, author.
Title: The Pig War and the Pelican Girls : 21 extraordinary and forgotten
    stories from American history / Joe Cuhaj.
Other titles: 21 extraordinary and forgotten stories from American history
Description: Essex, Connecticut : Prometheus, [2025] | Includes
    bibliographical references. | Summary: "Whether you're an armchair
    historian or a lover of all things unusual and astonishing, this
    collection of obscure history shows that life surely is stranger than
    fiction"— Provided by publisher.
Identifiers: LCCN 2024040393 (print) | LCCN 2024040394 (ebook) | ISBN
    9781493088270 (paperback) | ISBN 9781493088287 (epub)
Subjects: LCSH: United States—History—Anecdotes.
Classification: LCC E189 .C874 2025 (print) | LCC E189 (ebook) | DDC
    973.2—dc23/eng/20241129
LC record available at https://lccn.loc.gov/2024040393
LC ebook record available at https://lccn.loc.gov/2024040394

♾️™ The paper used in this publication meets the minimum requirements of
American National Standard for Information Sciences—Permanence of Paper
for Printed Library Materials, ANSI/NISO Z39.48-1992

*A generation which ignores history
has no past—and no future.*

—Robert A. Heinlein

CONTENTS

INTRODUCTION

History is much more than this happened on that date and that happened on this date. History is a journey where there are many forks in the road, twists and turns that often lead us to fascinating back alleys where the unexpected happens, and it surprises us.

The back alley of American history is what this book is all about. Sure, we know the basics of the Revolutionary War, the history of slavery before and during the Civil War, and so on. But underlying the basic facts are fascinating stories that are seldom told. Stories of heroic young girls who put their lives on the line to save a community during the War of 1812. The argument as to whether or not the United States has already had its first female president, although not elected by the people. The story of how the start of America's role in World War II caused a panic in one major US city so palpable that the residents and Civil Defense began shooting randomly at perceived targets that were not there. This is only a sample of the type of stories you will find within these pages.

I consider myself very fortunate in that I had some wonderful influences growing up that piqued my interest in history. Why I didn't pursue it as a career option, I have no idea. I take that back; it's probably because I had my heart set on becoming a radio announcer. But that's another story.

First and foremost, there was my family. Everyone—my mom, dad, sister—we all enjoyed learning about history. My mother and father could spout tidbits of historical facts at a moment's notice. Both my sister and I excelled in history courses throughout our public school years. And that brings me to my second influence: my history teachers at good old Mahwah High School in New Jersey.

I had some of the best teachers during my public school years, bringing what otherwise would be stodgy, boring history out of the dustbin and into the light, taking us down those back alleys to discover that there is much more to it than simply regurgitating facts and dates. They avoided painting history with broad strokes, instead, using a fine, thin brush to bring out something extraordinary about our nation's, and the world's, past. Classes were riveting.

In addition to basic English courses, Mahwah High School also offered amazing creative writing and journalism classes that juiced my love of writing. One teacher, Mr. Clough, really made an impression on me. While he shared countless historical facts and dates, he was more of a comedian. He never droned on and on about a subject; instead, he injected humor into his lectures with his Groucho Marx–like mustache, delivery, and puns. More importantly, Mr. Clough was a wealth of knowledge, tossing in fascinating, little-known, and obscure stories about whatever period in history we were studying. It was the history behind the history.

Then there were my reading habits. I must admit, I was a weird kid growing up in northern New Jersey, just outside of New York City in the 1960s. Living near the Big Apple meant one thing for our household: newspapers. Tons of newspapers, delivered either by the paperboy—flailing rolled-up papers onto the front lawn, coming precariously close to taking out a window as he weaved his bike down the street, one hand on the handlebars—or by me. Every Sunday I was sent on a mission by my dad to head downtown to the local newsstand and pick up the Sunday edition of the

Jersey-centric *Bergen Record*, the *Daily News*, and the Sunday *New York Times*. The latter was thick, about the size of three Manhattan phone books stacked one on top of the other (you remember phone books, don't you?).

The entire family would devour them all, endlessly, from front to back. The *Daily News* was extra special because it was one of the first papers in the country with pages and pages of glorious, full-color comics on Sunday. Naturally, you would think that a boy of ten or eleven would automatically gravitate toward those. Not me. (That's what made me a weird kid.)

I would grab the Sunday *Times* and head to the last section of the paper, maybe it was section "G," page 46, the very last pages. Here I would find obscure and offbeat news stories that fascinated me. They were no more than a short two or three paragraphs long, telling the reader about world and pop-culture events and the everyday lives of ordinary people from around the globe. They were stories that never made the headlines, sometimes tragic, sometimes heartwarming, sometimes just plain funny, and others that would leave you shaking your head, but they all painted a picture of what life was like during that time in history. Stories that have long since been lost to time.

And that is how I became an armchair historian, the voices of Mr. Clough and my family ringing in my ears all of these years, urging me on to write my five nonfiction history books, including my previous two Prometheus Books, *Space Oddities: Forgotten Stories of Mankind's Exploration of Space* and *Everyone's Gone to the Moon: July 1969, Life on Earth, and the Epic Voyage of Apollo 11*. The memories of how much I used to love discovering long-since-forgotten stories in the newspaper and the offbeat stories told in my high school history classes made me want to dig deep for stories that have been relegated to the dustbin of history.

As I was wrapping up *Everyone's Gone to the Moon*, I was flooded with visions of Mr. Clough, telling us tales of a war that almost started between the United States and Canada, all because of a pig being shot; of how during the Civil War, free Blacks in the South were so afraid for their lives that many relinquished their freedom and petitioned their local governments to become slaves, believing it was safer living and working on a plantation than being free; how two young girls in Massachusetts fooled the British navy during the Revolution and saved their town. And with that, the idea for *The Pig War and the Pelican Girls* was born.

My goal for this book is not to present you with a stodgy, stuffy, date-riddled history book. Instead, I want to share with you the excitement I felt when I discovered unusual tales from our country's past. I hope you will be surprised, amused, and perhaps a little shocked when you read the little-known and compelling tales of adventure, romance, espionage, and more from our fascinating past. I hope this book is only the beginning of your own adventure. There are plenty more such tales out there, lurking in the shadows, ready to be discovered if we only care to look for them.

Enjoy!

· 1 ·

THE PIG WAR

The islands of the Pacific Northwest are simply spectacular. The windswept rocky and rugged coastline of the archipelago along the border between the state of Washington and Vancouver, British Columbia, is topped with the dark green spires of Douglas fir, western hemlock, and red berry–laden madrone trees. The forests are spotted with grassy balds where brilliant wildflowers bloom in season. Harbor seals sun themselves along the shoreline, while giant black-and-white orcas playfully breach the surface of the surrounding waters.

Today, this idyllic landscape is the perfect vacation getaway for those looking to add a little adventure to their lives. Maybe it's kayaking with orcas, hiking through the beautiful red cedar and hemlock forest at Olympic National Park, or just sitting next to the water's edge for a stunning sunset, with plenty of peace and quiet. It is a vacationer's paradise, but it wasn't always this way. In fact, in the middle of the nineteenth century, one of the islands in the chain, San Juan Island, came as close as it possibly could to being the site of a full-fledged war between two of the world's great nations at the time—and it was all because of an incident concerning a pig.

San Juan Island was first inhabited by the Coast Salish peoples over ten thousand years ago, a group of forty independent nations that speak over twenty different languages. Europeans first arrived in the region around 1770, with Spanish explorers looking to expand the territory they already held in Northern California. It was an area that the British had already laid claim to. The overlapping of claims nearly resulted in a war between the two nations, but after negotiations, a peaceful accommodation was reached and official boundaries established. This lasted until 1819, when Spain relinquished all of their land, transferring its share of the Pacific Northwest to the fledgling United States, who established the city of Seattle while the British created the city of Vancouver.

In 1840, the British government officially added to its empire with the establishment of the Province of Canada, a sprawling collection of territories along a border north of the still-growing United States that stretched from the Atlantic to the Pacific. While most of the territory claimed by Britain was not in dispute, the San Juan archipelago, which consisted of well over 170 islands, was a different story. The largest of the islands, San Juan, was deemed to be of strategic importance to both the United States and Britain due to its location along the Salish Sea, which flowed directly into the Pacific Ocean. Both countries laid claim to the island, and soon thereafter, settlers began moving in.

In 1845, one of the world's largest trading companies at the time, the Hudson's Bay Company—which had established a large string of trading posts across the Pacific Northwest between 1820 and 1850—also laid claim to the island. Up to this point, both American and British settlers had been living together peacefully on the island, but it was becoming apparent that this quiet existence would not last long. A border needed to be established between the United States and Canada. Both countries sat down at the bargaining table, and in short order, hammered out an agreement. The Oregon Treaty, which went into effect on June 15, 1846, established the official border between the two countries: A line of latitude, the 49th parallel, would be the demarcation line. For the most part, this was the perfect solution, creating a long, solid border without having to divide rivers and lakes in half. At least, this was true until the border reached the San Juan Islands.

The treaty vaguely specified that the border at the archipelago would be in "the middle of the channel which separates the continent from Vancouver Island, and thence southerly through the middle of said channel." The word hardly describes that passage, because if you look on a map, the San Juan Islands have several channels, including the Haro and Rosario Straits that wind their way around the myriad islands. What was the treaty trying to say?

In 1851, the Hudson's Bay Company established a salmon-curing station on San Juan Island, but in 1853, the US government claimed the entire island as part of its growing Washington Territory. In retaliation, the Hudson's Bay Company, led by Charles Griffin, established a large sheep ranch, the Belle Vue Sheep Farm, on the island's 1,500-acre coastal prairie that had been previously established and maintained by the Coast Salish people. The farm quickly grew, with over 4,500 head of sheep grazing the grass by 1859, and also boasting thirty-five horses, forty cattle, and, most importantly for this story, forty hogs.

The farm was an enormous success and Americans took notice. Not only did the success of Belle Vue prove that the island had enormous potential for raising livestock, but basic agriculture could thrive there as well, and the number of Americans on the island started to grow. By late spring of 1859, eighteen Americans had staked claims to land on prime Hudson's Bay Company pastures. The British government considered these Yanks to be squatters, illegally trespassing and threatening the peace and tranquility of the island, and tensions began to mount between settlers of both nations.

Up until the summer of 1859, Charles Griffin's hogs had enjoyed a good life, roaming freely across the island, but in June, one of the hogs crossed into land that was claimed by American

Lyman Cutlar. Cutlar found the pig rooting through his potato crop. There was an unsubstantiated report that the two men had a "conversation" about the pig:

Cutlar: It was eating my potatoes!

Griffin: Rubbish. It's up to you to keep your potatoes out of my pig!

On June 15, Cutlar shot and killed the pig. Presumably feeling some remorse (and that's only a presumption), Griffin offered Cutlar $10 in compensation for the loss of his pig. That didn't appease the hog's owner, who was so outraged that he reported the incident to British authorities, who in turn threatened to arrest Cutlar, deeming that all Americans on San Juan Island were trespassers, and as such, threatened to forcibly remove them.

After filing his report, Griffin waited for action to be taken by the British government. Something had to be done to avenge the loss of his pig. Perhaps soldiers on the British ship stationed nearby, the HMS *Satellite*, could expel every last Yank from the island? Griffin went to bed that night fully expecting to wake up to the *Satellite* anchored off the coast, meaning the governor of nearby Vancouver Island, James Douglas, had fulfilled his request. But when he woke up, instead of seeing the Union Jack flying above a ship anchored offshore, he saw the American flag hoisted atop the USS *Massachusetts*. Not taking any chances, the Americans on the island had made their own request, asking the US government for protection. The ship offshore was their response.

On board the *Massachusetts* was the flamboyant Captain George E. Pickett, the same officer who would lead the famous Pickett's Charge at Gettysburg a few years later, during the Civil War. On July 27, Pickett and his sixty-four-man Company D of the 9th US Infantry landed on the island and made camp just north of the Belle Vue Sheep Farm.

Upon Pickett's landing, Governor Douglas ordered the Royal Navy's frigate, HMS *Tribune*, with its thirty-one cannons, under the command of Captain Geoffrey Phipps Hornby, along with the HMS *Satellite* and the HMS *Plumper*, to move into position and remove Pickett and his men from the island, refraining from the use of force, if possible. Over the next month, Hornby was able to reinforce his troops, but refused to take any military action to remove Pickett's army, or to remove any Americans.

Pickett did not feel threatened by the increase in British military might, and responded by landing additional men to his encampment on the island. By August, the eight 32-pound cannons from the USS *Massachusetts* were removed from the ship and placed in a hastily built redoubt onshore.

The threat of war was escalating exponentially. By this time, the British had a total of five warships situated off the coast and one thousand marines at the ready. Captain Hornby, still under orders not to use force against the Americans, began showing some muscle, demonstrating the might of the British navy by conducting live drills, firing shots from their fifty-two cannons into the island's rocky shores. Tourists from nearby islands and the town of Vancouver on the mainland sailed over to San Juan in droves to watch the spectacle that was unfolding. Still, Hornby would not directly engage the Americans until the commander of British naval forces in the Pacific, Rear Admiral Robert Lambert Baynes, arrived to assess the situation and provide further orders.

As cannonballs were being lobbed at the shoreline by the British navy's cannons, the Americans were reinforcing, and by August 31, they had 461 soldiers on the island, with a total of twenty-two cannons. The situation was quickly getting out of hand. It appeared that it would take only the slightest provocation, intentional or not, by either the United States or Britain, and the two nations would be at war once again, just forty-four years after the end of the War of 1812—only this time it would not be over political disputes or philosophical reasons. This time it would be over the killing of a pig.

With a shooting war seemingly inevitable, cooler heads finally prevailed. Rear Admiral Baynes finally arrived on the island, and despite intense pressure from Vancouver Island's governor, he refused to order an attack on the Americans, saying, "[I] will not involve two great nations in a war over a squabble about a pig."

At the same time, word of the "Pig War" had made it to the desk of President James Buchanan in Washington. Buchanan dispatched the commander of the US Army, General Winfield Scott, to the scene to negotiate an agreement to end the conflict. Upon Scott's arrival, an agreement was quickly reached that would allow one contingent of soldiers from each side to remain on the island: One would establish what would be called the American Camp on the south side of the island, while the British Camp would be established on the northwest side.

War had been averted, and both sides lived peacefully together, respecting the agreement for the next twelve years. With the signing of the Treaty of Washington in 1871 by the United States and Britain, the issue of who controlled the island was left to an international arbitrator, Prussian king and German emperor Kaiser Wilhelm I. He established a three-man arbitration committee that would settle for the last time the borders between the two nations around islands of the Pacific Northwest. On October 21, 1872, the committee ruled that the boundary between the United States and Canada in the San Juan Island chain would be down the center of Haro Strait, which meant that San Juan Island would now belong to the United States.

British troops abandoned their camp on November 25, 1872. American troops left in July 1874. Just over one hundred years after the Pig War incident, the US government established the San Juan Island National Historical Park. Under the management of the National Park Service, visitors today can walk or ride bikes around the island to view the spectacular wildlife and incredible views. They can also visit the sites of the American and British Camps, where two great nations nearly went to battle over the killing of a pig.

FOOTNOTE TO HISTORY: THE QUASI-WAR

In 1778, the fledgling United States signed its first international agreements, the Treaty of Amity and Commerce and the Treaty of Alliance, with France. When the rebellion against the British monarchy began in the United States three years earlier, the French government under the reign of King Louis XVI sided with the rebellious colonies and began trading with them. The two agreements signed in 1778 took that relationship one step further by officially forming a military alliance between the two nations. They also affirmed that France recognized the United States as an independent country and required that the United States and France would have to both agree to any peace agreements with the British before they could be signed.

Trouble arose between the two nations following the overthrow of King Louis during the French Revolution in 1789, five years after the Revolutionary War had ended. The newly formed French Directory was angered when the United States signed the Jay Treaty with Britain in 1794, which cleared up a series of previously unresolved issues stemming from the Revolution and generally normalized relations between the two nations. One of those unresolved issues was allowing the United States to begin trading freely with Britain and its Caribbean colonies.

When the treaty was signed, across the Atlantic Ocean, the newly formed French government was at war with several European countries, including Britain. When the United States declared that it would be neutral in the French war against Britain, the French government became incensed. The declaration of neutrality flew in the face of the previous treaty agreed upon by the United States and France in 1778.

In retaliation, the French government issued an order that allowed for their naval vessels to seize any American merchant ship they came across, effectively treating the United States as an enemy. Between 1796 and 1797, over three hundred US merchant ships and their cargo were seized by French privateers. In response, the United States withheld any payments it owed France, accrued during the Revolution.

Tensions began to boil over. In November 1798, one of the first US Navy ships, the USS *Retaliation*, spotted what they thought was a friendly British ship on the horizon, but by the time they got close enough for a good look, the crew realized the ship they had spotted was French. By then it was too late to attack, and the *Retaliation* became the first US Navy ship to surrender without a single shot being fired by either side. Not long after, the USS *Constitution* encountered the same ship that had captured the *Retaliation*. The ship fired off a few shots, and the French ship surrendered.

With only sixteen ships in the newly minted US Navy, it is quite impressive to think that the American navy captured eighty-six French privateers in one year. War was never declared between the two nations, which earned this event in American history the moniker, the "Quasi-War." While not a recognized conflict, it served as an end to hostilities between the United States, Britain, and France for twelve years, before the beginning of the War of 1812.

· 2 ·

THE TALE OF THE
PELICAN GIRLS

The history of human habitation along the American Gulf
Coast—specifically, the northern Gulf Coast in and around
Mobile Bay, and the second-largest river delta in the country, the
Mobile–Tensaw River Delta in Alabama—is a rather complicated
and choreographed story between nations. Over the years, the area
has been claimed by Native Americans, Spain, France, England,
and Spain again, before becoming part of the United States.

The bay and delta that made this human habitation possible
is an incredibly fertile region with a myriad of freshwater rivers,
streams, and marshes flowing southward before emptying into the
Gulf of Mexico. The region is rife with flora and fauna. The wide
bay and expansive river delta are prone to extensive flooding, which
pushes the rich nutrients in the water over the banks, making the
soil perfect for growing a variety of crops.

The region in and around the bay and delta was first inhabited by Native Americans as far back as AD 1000, with one tribe,
the Mabila, proving to be highly successful in establishing per-
manent settlements there. Known as "mound builders," the tribe
built towering earthen mounds by digging one basket full of dirt
at a time by hand, using shell hoes, then piling the dirt up in the

center of the settlement, creating mounds as tall as 45 feet. Tribal leaders and religious figures would reside and hold ceremonies atop these mounds. The tribe's name would eventually be anglicized to "Mobile" when Europeans arrived, for which the bay and future city would eventually be named.

The first European to venture into this new land was Spanish explorer Alonso Álvarez, who sailed along the Gulf Coast looking for locations to create new settlements for Spain. Álvarez came to the bay in 1519 and began a survey of the rich landscape. His exploration resulted in Spain establishing several settlements along the northern Gulf Coast, including along the banks of Mobile Bay and its feeding rivers and creeks. Most of these failed and were left vacant, except for one of note—a settlement to the east of the bay that would later be called "Pensacola," in what the Spaniards called "New Florida."

It would be almost two hundred years after Alvarez arrived on the scene that the story of the Pelican Girls begins. In the late 1600s, the French began exploring the Gulf Coast of this new land and discovered that Spain had all but vanished from the scene. The French established a settlement in what would later become Biloxi, Mississippi, but a yellow fever outbreak devastated the settlement, and it was temporarily abandoned.

In 1700, while charting the coastline of the Gulf of Mexico for the French government, cartographer Claude Delisle sailed up the shallow waters of Mobile Bay and entered the delta. What he found was a paradise, a virtual Garden of Eden. In his journal, *Voyage de M. de Sauvole du fort des Bilochies ou Maurepas aux Thomies, sur la differentes fois* ("A Voyage to the Mobile and Tomeh"), he wrote:

> *The river divides into three branches at the boundary of their lands [the Thomees], and makes two islands which are very beautiful, and deserted in several places. This place is adorned with beautiful peach*

trees that are covered in fruit, but I do not know the quality they are since they were still green. There are also grapes which cover the banks of the river.

Two years later, in 1702, Jean-Baptiste Le Moyne de Bienville and his brother, Pierre Le Moyne d'Iberville, moved the settlement in Biloxi eastward to Mobile Bay. The brothers sailed approximately 27 miles up the shallow waters of the bay, entered the Mobile River, and established a crude fort along the banks of the river. The rudimentary outpost was named after the king of France, Fort Louis de la Mobile, or Fort Louis de la Louisiane.

While the river, delta, and bay were prime locations for establishing a new colony, it also had its challenges. This area of the Gulf had a subtropical climate, which meant that the colonists fought extreme heat and humidity. The waters around the fort were teeming with alligators, and mosquitoes swarmed in the swamps and marshes. Despite these hardships, the settlers continued to make a go of it, many being spurred on by the rumor that hidden somewhere in this "paradise" were untold riches. Instead of working the fields and building up the settlement, these settlers preferred searching for the legendary gold.

The French government deemed it much too dangerous to send women and children to a new land, so the first colonists to arrive in Mobile were basically all men. Having very few women in the new settlement made it almost impossible to foster population growth, and without female companionship, many of the male colonists (known as *coureurs de bois*, or "runners of the woods") began having relations with women from nearby Native American tribes, much to the chagrin of Bienville.

Not long after the fort was established, Bienville wrote to King Louis XIV several times, urging him to send women to the colony in order to foster a sustainable population.

*If you want to make something of this country, it is absolutely neces-
sary to send this year some families and a few girls who will be married off shortly after arrival.*

The king was reluctant to fulfill the request. He had been down
this road before and had been burned when he sent women to be
brides for male colonists in the newly formed French colony of
Martinique in the Caribbean. Between the years 1680 and 1685,
250 girls were sent to the island. These women had "questionable
backgrounds," many having been prostitutes, and were described
as being "poor creatures." Upon their arrival, the women were presented to single men by displaying them on a platform and auc-
tioning them off to the highest bidder in what became known as
the "white women trade." Many of the women refused to marry
the men who had purchased them after the auction was completed.
Bienville remembered this history as well and stressed in his letters
that the women sent to Fort Louis had to be "suitable women."

After much prodding, the king relented. At the time, France
was embroiled with Britain in what was known as Queen Anne's
War, so with a shortage of manpower and a vow to not make
the Martinique mistake again, the king turned to the Catholic
Church to begin the process. His instructions were to find women
that were virgins, with character beyond reproach, and with no
family or prospects for starting a family in the future in Europe.

Under the supervision of the bishop of Quebec, Monsignor
Vallier, the Church began canvassing convents, looking for suitable women to sail to the new settlement. To be considered, the
young ladies would have to be from good families, sit for rigorous
interviews, and produce a letter of recommendation proving
that their character was of the highest standards. In the end,
twenty-three young women ranging in age from fourteen to nineteen were promised husbands and a glorious life in what was described to them as a Garden of Eden.

In October 1703, the twenty-three women selected climbed aboard horse-drawn carriages and made the arduous 300-mile ride from Paris to the French seaport of Rochefort. In Rochefort, the girls, along with Father Henri de la Vente (the newly appointed pastor of the Mobile parish), Monsignor Vallier, three additional priests, and four nuns, would board the ship *Pelican* and along with two escort ships, the *Charente* and *Renommée*, to protect them from British warships, set sail for the new colony.

Queen Anne's War, however, caused the warship *Rochefort* to arrive late, and the *Pelican*'s passengers were forced to wait several months before departing. During that time, rumors about the new colony began to spread among the women. While they had been promised a new life in this so-called paradise, with the chance to marry one of the brave French patriots, instead they heard that the colonists were barbarians, living in poverty—that the fort was in a state of squalor, a haven for disease. Some of the women began to rethink the offer and wanted to back out, but when King Louis sweetened the deal by offering the women additional gifts and a substantial allowance, they changed their minds.

The *Pelican* finally set sail, but without its escort ships, its first stop being the French seaport of La Rochelle. The ship was delayed several more weeks before it finally began its journey to Fort Louis on April 19, 1704. From that moment on, the group of young women heading to Mobile would be known by the name of the ship they sailed on: the Pelican Girls.

The ship's first port of call would be the French colony of Cap-Haïtien, Haiti, in the Caribbean, a much-needed respite after the long sea voyage, during which many of the girls fell ill. Only a scant 30 miles from the island, the ship ran into a vicious squall and nearly capsized. Father de la Vente wrote, "We almost perished in the storm."

After spending some time in Haiti, the *Pelican* left port and headed to its next destination, Havana, Cuba. Arriving on July 7,

1704, the bishop of Cuba, Diego Evelino Hurtado de Compostela, greeted the girls and gave them decent lodging, introduced them to Caribbean delicacies, and took them on a personal tour of the city. The *Pelican* departed Havana on July 14, 1704, and headed north to the Gulf Coast and the Spanish-controlled colony at Pensacola, which was approximately 60 miles east of the mouth of Mobile Bay. The ship was denied entry into the city but was allowed to anchor offshore, where the colony sent supplies to the ship.

Finally, after a week anchored offshore, the *Pelican* set sail for its final destination, an island at the mouth of Mobile Bay known as Massacre Island (known today as Dauphin Island). By now, a little gift from the island of Cuba had reared its ugly head and was taking a toll on the crew and passengers. While in Cuba, they had been subjected to swarms of mosquitoes which, unbeknownst at the time, carried the dreaded yellow fever. By the time the *Pelican* had reached Massacre Island, half of the crew and several of the girls had died from the disease. Yellow fever would run rampant across the entire Gulf Coast for the next century.

Due to the shallowness of Mobile Bay, the girls disembarked from the *Pelican* and boarded shallow-draft boats to make the final journey to the French fort in Mobile. They finally arrived on August 1, 1704. According to Professor Charles Gayarré in his book, *History of Louisiana*, the colonists were puzzled when the women first stepped off the boat. They didn't understand why they were there, but that soon changed:

> *[The] excitement became intense when the inhabitants saw a procession of females with veiled faces proceeding arm in arm and two by two to the house of the governor, who received them in state and provided them with suitable lodgings.*

The colonists' questions about these new arrivals were answered the following morning by a priest who read an announcement that had accompanied the *Pelican* to Mobile:

His Majesty sends by that ship 20 girls to be married to the Canadians and others who have begun habitations at Mobile in order that this colony can firmly establish itself. Each of these girls was raised in virtue and piety and knows how to work, which will render them useful in the colony by showing the Indian girls what they can do, for this there being no point in sending other than [those] of virtue known and without reproach.

The women must have been sorely disappointed when they stepped off the boats. This was not the Garden of Eden they had been promised. The fort itself was not a fort, per se. Instead, it was a collection of dilapidated shacks with dirt floors surrounded by pools of stagnant water in ditches that were teeming with mosquitoes. The women also soon learned about the men's poor work ethic, and that there was a severe food shortage. The women found themselves relegated to eating Indian corn and acorns.

There were no prearranged marriages for the girls, and unlike in Martinique, where the women were auctioned off, each of the Pelican Girls was allowed to choose their future husband. In fact, before leaving France, the women had been armed with information about each potential suitor, including their background and financial situation. The women could then choose their own husband from the fifty or so bachelors.

It wasn't long before weddings were being held. According to historical accounts, there would be a courtship and an engagement period, followed by a wedding ceremony, all of which were conducted by Father de la Vente. Courtships and engagements must have been very short, however, since it was recorded that ceremonies were held on almost a daily basis during the first month after the Pelican Girls' arrival. By the end of the month, all—except one, which we'll get to in a moment—were married.

The women began life in the new colony, making the best of a bad situation. Disillusioned but determined, the Pelican Girls demonstrated great resolve to ensure that their fortunes would turn. At one point, the women united to stage what would later become known as the Petticoat Rebellion, revolting against their lazy husbands, denying them food and kicking them out of their homes until they got the message and began providing for the women.

The rebellion worked, but changes were slow in coming, with conditions in the new settlement still appalling. The women, now feeling strength in numbers, brought their grievances to Bienville, who became frustrated and infuriated with the women, calling them "pampered city girls." The situation prompted Bienville to write to the king and demand that next time, he send "hardworking country girls."

Along with the Pelican Girls, the ship had also brought another passenger from France, a midwife named Catherine Moulois. Sadly, only months after arriving, Catherine died, and the duty of midwife for the colony fell to Marie Grissot. Grissot attended the birth of the first child in the new colony to survive, a boy, to François and Anne LeMay, on October 22, 1704.

In the end, most of the girls married except for one, Françoise du Boisrenaud. According to the story—as told by the Wayne Saucier family, descendants of the Pelican Girls—the cousin of Bienville and lieutenant to the king, Pierre Boisbriant, asked Françoise to marry him. Bienville, for whatever reason, forbade the marriage. Instead, the founder of Mobile insisted that the young woman marry another man that he had chosen for her. Françoise refused, and the infuriated Bienville shot off a letter to the governor of the Louisiana colonies, demanding that the governor command Françoise to marry the man he had chosen for her. Once again she refused, and once again, Bienville became angry and wrote a terse letter to the king's colonial minister, Jérôme Phélypeaux, comte de Pontchartrain, demanding that he intervene and force Françoise to marry the man Bienville had chosen for her. Pontchartrain denied the request, but for whatever reason, after all of the commotion,

Françoise and her chosen husband, Pierre, never married. Perhaps it was to put the controversy to rest once and for all. In any event, Françoise remained in the settlement but never married.

An interesting bit of information was brought to my attention when I first wrote about the Pelican Girls. It is a tantalizing story that comes to us from a book written by Elizabeth Hammond in 1819, titled *Modern Domestic Cookery and Useful Recipe Book*. Hammond states that during their stay in the Caribbean, the Pelican Girls acquired a unique vegetable that was up to that point unknown in the New World. It was called "guingombo" or "kingombo"; today, we call it okra.

According to Hammond, when the girls arrived in Fort Louis de la Mobile, Bienville's housekeeper, Madame Langlois, cooked a fish stew for the girls. She tossed in locally sourced seafood and vegetables that were grown by local Indian tribes. The girls offered Langlois their okra for the stew, and the housekeeper added a touch of the French spice, filé powder. The result was what Hammond believed to be the first documented gumbo to be cooked and served in the New World.

Several years after the arrival of the Pelican Girls, the original French settlement in Biloxi was reestablished, and in 1719, a new group of women sailed into that colony just as the Pelican Girls had in Mobile. For a number of years, Fort Louis de la Mobile was the capital of the French Louisiana territory. The capital was eventually moved to a new French colony, New Orleans, after its founding in 1718.

In 1728, another ship sailed from France to New Orleans with yet another group of women destined to become wives to the colonists there. These women carried small wooden boxes that the French government had provided, called *casquettes*. Each box held what little precious possessions the girls were allowed to bring with them, which led to their sobriquet of "Casket Girls."

But this fascinating tale of France colonizing the New World all began with the Pelican Girls of Mobile. To this day, many Mobile residents proudly proclaim that their roots stem back to this intrepid group of young women.

FOOTNOTE TO HISTORY: AMERICA'S OLDEST CITY IS . . .

Fair warning, the following is a trick question: What is America's oldest city?

As the Florida Department of Tourism and the University of West Florida Historic Trust will tell you, it all depends on how you look at it. It could be either Pensacola on the Florida Panhandle, on the Gulf Coast, or St. Augustine on its Atlantic coast.

There is no debating that St. Augustine is the oldest continuously occupied European-settled city in America. It was established fifty-five years before the *Mayflower* landed at Plymouth Rock, and forty-two years before the British settled the colony of Jamestown in what would later become the state of Virginia. The Spanish laid claim to what became known as St. Augustine in 1565, and it has been inhabited ever since. According to city historians, explorer Don Pedro Menéndez de Avilés first set foot on the future settlement on September 8, 1565, to the cheers of the six hundred voyagers who had arrived with him. The city was named after the patron saint of brewers, theologians, and printers.

Pensacola, on the other hand, was actually first settled six years prior, in 1559, by conquistador

Tristan de Luna and a contingent of 1,400 people. After years of plying the waters of the Gulf of Mexico, searching for a suitable site for a new settlement (Pensacola was first identified as a possible site in 1513 by Ponce de León), de Luna chose Ochuse Bay, which is known today as Pensacola Bay.

De Luna immediately set about establishing a colony there. All seemed well at the settlement until the night of September 19, 1559, when a tremendous hurricane struck the region, lasting a solid twenty-four hours. The entire settlement and de Luna's fleet of eleven ships were completely destroyed. Survivors attempted to rebuild, but mosquitoes, disease, and attacks from local Native tribes forced them to abandon the site in 1561. The king of Spain, Philip II, deemed Florida too dangerous to settle, and no further settlements were established until St. Augustine in 1565. Pensacola was eventually resurrected and became a functioning settlement in 1698.

So, Pensacola was the first European settlement in what would eventually become the United States, but St. Augustine is the first continuously occupied, and both cities are understandably proud of the role they played in American history.

By the way, just off the coast of Pensacola, three of Tristan de Luna's ships that sank during that massive 1559 hurricane have been discovered by archaeology professors and students at the University of West Florida, an incredible historic find from the first attempt at settling and taming this New World.

· 3 ·

THEY DIDN'T GET
THE MEMO

Imagine you are in a fierce battle for your country and the causes
you believe in. When the battle ends, your side may be victorious,
or maybe not, but just after the battle ends and the smoke clears,
you receive word that the war had already ended while you were
still firing at the enemy. What would that do to one's thinking?
Would you wonder if it had been a futile effort and a waste of
time, money, and lives? Would you just be happy to know the war
had ended? And if you had lost and were forced to surrender the
territory you had just fought so valiantly for, what would your
reaction be? It would be difficult to shrug your shoulders and say
"Oh, well."

Such a scenario was commonplace in the not-too-distant past:
two warring countries fighting it out on a battlefield, or at sea,
only to find out after the smoke had cleared that the war was already over. It was back in the days when communication was slow
to arrive on a battlefield. There was no radio, no telephones. Only
messengers sent by sea across the oceans or by courier on horseback, or even slower, on foot.

Several significant battles have taken place either just as a major
war was ending or shortly thereafter. Two of the most notable were

fought along the Gulf Coast in Alabama and Louisiana during—or actually, *after*—the War of 1812 had ended.

In April 1813, during the War of 1812 along the Gulf Coast, the United States received word that Spain had evacuated the city of Mobile and had relocated east, to the city of Pensacola, leaving Mobile void of any military presence. Quickly, US colonel James Wilkinson swooped in with his troops and took control of the city, thus opening access to the Gulf of Mexico for Americans.

On the south end of the wide Mobile Bay, where the Bay meets the Gulf, there is a long sandy peninsula that juts out, acting as almost a natural demarcation line between the Gulf and the Bay. Wilkinson's men hastily built a redoubt of earth and wood on the beach at the tip of the peninsula, at Mobile Point, to protect the Bay from being infiltrated by the Royal Navy. By the summer, the completed redoubt was approximately 22,000 square feet in size, with a 400-foot semicircular exterior wall that was named for the fort's first commander, Colonel John Bowyer.

During the construction of the fort, a report appeared in the May 26, 1813, edition of the *Daily National Intelligencer* that warned of possible danger on the horizon from those "who might be hovering off the coast." They were talking about King George III's Royal Navy.

Britain had one goal in mind, and that was to gain control of Mobile, which it could then use as a base to attack and capture New Orleans. British naval captain William Percy planned to land a contingent of soldiers just east of the newly built Fort Bowyer, which was manned by 160 men from the 2nd US Infantry. These troops would march in and attack the fort from the east while Percy's fleet attacked from the Gulf of Mexico. With a victory here, Percy would then set sail and take New Orleans.

On September 12, 1814, Percy landed a battalion of 225 royal marines and Native Americans 9 miles east of the fort on the narrow, sandy peninsula, and two days later, the troops attacked the fort by land, while off the coast, the HMS *Hermes*, HMS *Sophie*, HMS *Childers*, and HMS *Carron* positioned themselves and began to open fire.

Only two hours after the shelling of the fort began, the *Hermes* ran aground directly in front of the fort's gun ports. Captain Percy was forced to scuttle the ship and call off the attack. It was quite an impressive win by the small group of American soldiers manning the fort. It also caused Percy to rethink his plans and send his ships directly to attack New Orleans. If Britain could take that city, it would be a huge victory, since it would give the British control of the mighty Mississippi River, an important commercial route for the United States that saw one-third of its produce shipped downstream to the city and then off to trading partners around the world.

Major General Andrew Jackson knew what was about to happen, and on November 22, 1814, he left Mobile and headed west to New Orleans. Along the route his troops were joined by militia from Tennessee and Kentucky. Jackson and his men arrived in New Orleans on December 1. Meanwhile, British forces, under the command of Admiral Sir Alexander Cochrane, had arrived just off the coast, and on December 14, began bombarding Jackson and his men. After destroying several American gunboats, Cochrane was in control of Lake Borgne and edged closer to the city, landing his men at Villere Plantation just south of New Orleans.

But Jackson wasn't defeated just yet. On December 23, with the aid of cannon fire from the USS *Carolina*, Jackson ordered his men to open fire. The attack took the British completely off guard, and ten minutes later, Jackson ordered the men to rush the British lines. It was a fierce battle that lasted until the sun began to set. The bayous were almost invisible due to the amount of smoke from the guns and cannons that filled the air, so much so that both sides disengaged.

Jackson's troops dug in after dropping back to the Rodriguez Canal on the Chalmette Plantation. In the meantime, peace negotiations had concluded between the two nations, and on Christmas Eve, 1814, the Treaty of Ghent was signed, ending the war. But communications being the way they were back then, it would take weeks for commanders and their troops to receive the news. With that, on New Year's Day, 1815, the British picked up where they had left off and began a sustained and ferocious bombardment of what became known as Line Jackson. When the guns finally fell silent, the British decided to attempt a full-on infantry assault on the Americans.

At first light on January 8, the British made the move toward Line Jackson, but the gunfire from the Americans was too much. In twenty minutes, the British lost two thousand men. They called a hasty retreat, and the United States had their biggest victory of the war, even though it had already ended. Andrew Jackson became a national hero, eventually becoming the country's seventh president.

But the Battle of New Orleans wasn't the last fight of the war. Once again, it would take place at Fort Bowyer.

Fearing another attack on the fort, General Jackson ordered more troops to Fort Bowyer, increasing the contingent to 375 men, along with twenty-eight cannons. As it turns out, Jackson was right. On February 7, 1815, Percy's ships returned and began a heavy bombardment of Fort Bowyer. The following day, a contingent of British soldiers marched from a position 7 miles east of the fort and began a ground attack.

The men of Fort Bowyer held out for five days under intense cannon fire and bombing before they finally surrendered the peninsula. It looked as though the British would be able to sail right in and take over Mobile without any resistance. But, as we know, the war had already ended. Word finally arrived on the scene that the War of 1812 was finally over. The British were forced to withdraw from the peninsula, returning the fort and the land they had captured in that last battle back to the Americans.

Warfare was completely transformed in 1844 when inventor Samuel Morse invented the telegraph. It wasn't long before poles had sprung up across America with telegraph wires sprawling across the landscape. During the Civil War itself, it is estimated that the US military strung over 15,000 miles of telegraph wire to bolster its war effort. President Lincoln became the first president to use this new form of mechanical communication to track the progress of the war and issue orders to the troops. As documentarian Ken Burns tells us in his award-winning *The Civil War*, it also gave the president a new headache: how to manage the media, who could also get news of the war quickly, delivering it to the daily newspapers over those same telegraph wires.

The date was April 9, 1865. The Civil War was not yet technically over, even as General Lee was surrendering the Army of the Potomac to General Ulysses S. Grant at Appomattox Courthouse, Virginia, but the writing was on the wall. As the two met and signed the instrument of surrender, there was one more major battle taking place along the Gulf Coast, at a fort on the eastern shore of Mobile Bay, across from Mobile, the last Confederate port city standing. While the war was virtually over—there were still many other Rebel armies that needed to surrender—this is one final battle that had a most unusual ending.

With the fall of every other port city of the Confederacy—New Orleans, Pensacola, Charleston, and so on—Mobile was the last remaining port, and became an important target for the Union, as pointed out by *New York Times* reporter Benjamin Clay:

Mobile, as I before informed you, is now next to Richmond, the best fortified city in the Southern Confederacy. It has long been an eye sore to us, and some time ago—in fact, immediately after the battle of Nashville—the great military eye of the republic was turned this way.

At the southern end of Mobile Bay was Fort Morgan, one of a series of stone fortresses the federal government had built across the country following the War of 1812. It was constructed on the site of the former Fort Bowyer, and under the control of Confederate troops; however, the men were losing patience, and their appetite for war. Many were deserting. A reporter with the *Boston Journal* filed this report about the morale of the men at the fort:

The deserters bring the very important intelligence that the rebel army in and around Mobile have organized secret societies, and determined to fight no longer. It is said that the movement inaugurated among the soldiers is growing daily stronger and many officers are compromised in the movement.

Nevertheless, those soldiers had one more battle to fight. On the morning of August 5, 1864, the US warship the USS *Hartford*, under the command of Union admiral David Farragut, positioned his fleet of eighteen ships near Fort Morgan. On his orders, the fleet began sailing north from the Gulf of Mexico into Mobile Bay. The admiral positioned his ironclads so that they would run between Fort Morgan and his wooden ships, to protect them from cannon fire.

The waters around the fort were heavily fortified. Confederate soldiers had driven large wooden pilings into the shoals far out into the bay, up to the main shipping channel, in order to prevent unsuspecting Union ships from sneaking up the bay. The fort had twenty-four cannons, and the Confederate navy's largest and most powerful ironclad, the CSS *Tennessee*, was stationed just offshore.

The most important defense against a Union invasion by sea were the mines, or as they were called in 1864, torpedoes, which were placed strategically offshore. These weapons consisted of lacquer-coated wooden kegs and cone-shaped metal barrels packed with up to 50 pounds of black powder and armed with primers; when struck by a ship, they would explode.

The Battle of Mobile Bay began at dawn, with one Confederate soldier describing the sound of the cannons as being "one continuous peal of thunder, deafening to the extreme."

Farragut climbed up onto the rigging of the *Hartford* and watched the progress of his fleet. To his horror, the ironclad USS *Tecumseh* had veered off course to pursue the *Tennessee*. The *Tecumseh* struck a mine, which exploded. Quickly, the ship rolled over and sank to the shallow bottom of the Bay, killing ninety-two crew members, including her captain.

Seeing the disaster, Farragut steeled his determination and allegedly gave an order that rallied his fleet and became a battle cry for future generations of navy commanders: "Damn the torpedoes! Full speed ahead!"

The battle raged on for three hours before the *Tennessee* had a hole blown in its side. Soon after, Confederate admiral Franklin Buchanan ran up the white flag and surrendered the vessel.

Having secured the Bay, the city of Mobile was next. Two divisions of Union troops moved inland from the south and east from Pensacola, Florida, heading for a small Confederate fort located only 5 miles east of Mobile on the opposite side of the bay, Fort Blakeley.

After a hard slog through swamps and heavy rain, 16,000 federal troops finally descended on Fort Blakeley and began battling 3,500 Confederate soldiers on April 2, 1865. Many Rebels on the Confederate line turned and ran. Some simply surrendered. Others stayed and fought in a fierce close-quarters battle. In the end, 75 Confederate soldiers were killed as compared to 150 US soldiers. On April 9, the war ended, as Lee surrendered to Grant. Two days later, Mobile mayor R. H. Sloane surrendered the city.

When it came to Southern cities, Mobile was one of the lucky ones. Federal troops crossed the Bay and took control of the city without any resistance. There were no skirmishes, no buildings burned. The city was left intact, virtually undisturbed by the war. But in an ironic twist of fate, a sizable portion of the city was destroyed shortly after its surrender.

As the Union Army marched into town, arms and munitions were surrendered by Confederate soldiers. These were gathered up and placed in storage in a riverside warehouse, Marshall's, at the corner of Lipscomb and Commercial Streets. One month after the surrender of the city and the end of the war, the munitions in the building ignited. Twenty tons of explosives exploded. Newspapers reported that eight city blocks were destroyed in the blast, an enormous crater all that was left in the spot where buildings once stood. Fires destroyed the entire north section of the city, as well as eight thousand bales of hay that were stored in adjacent warehouses. The steamers *Cowles* and *Kate Dale* that were docked along the city's waterfront were hit hard by the concussion and sank, with all on board.

In an act of peaceful bipartisanship, both Mobilians and federal troops jumped in to put out the fires, rescue survivors, and save whatever they could of the waterfront. When all was said and done, it was estimated that three hundred people were killed, with scores wounded. The city that was untouched by the battles of war had still lost a major battle without a shot being fired.

One month before the Battle of Blakeley and the surrender of Lee to Grant, along the Rio Grande River in Texas near Brownsville, a gentleman's agreement was reached between Union and Confederate troops to cease hostilities. By May of 1865, however, despite the agreement, and after receiving word of Lee's surrender, Union colonel Theodore H. Barrett decided that he wanted to take out the Confederate encampments that were still in the region.

On May 11, Barrett dispatched a regiment of five hundred soldiers from his camp at Brazos Santiago, Texas, to several Confederate encampments scattered around the area, with every intention of attacking those camps. Three hundred of those under the command of Lieutenant Colonel David Branson made their way to White and Palmito Ranches.

When the army arrived at White Ranch, they found no Confederate troops stationed there. After securing the ranch, Benson marched his troops to Palmito Ranch, but as they approached, they were spotted by the Texas cavalry battalion stationed there, and a skirmish broke out between the two armies. It was a short fight, with both sides retreating by nightfall.

Overnight, Benson requested reinforcements, and by morning, two hundred additional soldiers joined his company. Union troops now outnumbered the Confederates, five hundred to three hundred, when the second attack began. After a few hours, the Confederates ordered up their own reinforcements, and soon an additional four hundred men rallied around the Rebel commander and began a counterattack. After a long and sustained bombardment, the Confederate troops came close to capturing Benson's army, but an escape route was still open, and the Union troops fled the scene, thus ending the last battle of the Civil War.

Or was it?

The Confederacy had many obstacles to conquer if it were ever to fully become an independent country. Military funding, severe rationing on the home front, and hit-and-miss victories on the battlefield made gaining the upper hand in the war challenging. This was not the case at sea, where their navy was literally built from scratch, and they were able to recruit a small but effective privateer fleet. The latter destroyed or captured hundreds of US ships, which forced the Union to transfer almost 800,000 tons of shipping cargo to foreign ships for safe transport across the Atlantic. The attacks by the Confederate raiders, also known as commerce raiders, caused insurance premiums for Union ships to skyrocket, making shipping goods a costly proposition.

First launched in River Clyde, Scotland, on August 17, 1863, as the *Sea King*, the ship was purchased by the Confederacy in 1864 and renamed the CSS *Shenandoah*. The ship was an iron-framed vessel with auxiliary steam power. During its time in service, the *Shenandoah* was one of the more successful raiders. Between 1864 and 1865, the vessel captured or sank thirty-eight Union merchant ships, its first being the *Alina* out of Maine that was shipping railway iron to Buenos Aires. The final shot taken by the *Shenandoah* at a merchant ship was recorded by the ship's master mate as being fired by gunner John L. Guy on June 22, 1865, two months after Lee's surrender. The shot was taken at the whaler *New Bedford* in Alaska's Bering Sea.

The *Shenandoah*, under the command of Lieutenant James Iredell Waddell, was continuing its voyages out in the Pacific Ocean when on August 2, 1865, she became the last Confederate ship to receive word that the war had ended three months earlier.

Waddell and his crew knew they would surely be arrested and hanged for treason if they returned home. After hearing of how Captain Raphael Semmes and the crew of the CSS *Alabama* had surrendered and received clemency in England, Waddell made the decision to do the same. He had the ship's cannons removed, lowered the Confederate flag, and set sail for Liverpool, England, all the while being pursued by US naval vessels.

The *Shenandoah* arrived on November 6, 1865, but without flying a flag of any nation, the harbor pilot would not let the ship enter. Once again, Waddell raised the Confederate flag, which satisfied the harbor pilot, and the captain of the British naval vessel, HMS *Donegal*, accepted the last surrender of the Civil War. In doing so, the British government declared that the ship and crew were to be paroled and allowed to come ashore.

As it turns out, the *Shenandoah* not only made history as the final surrender of the Civil War; she was also the only Confederate naval ship to circumnavigate the world.

FOOTNOTE TO HISTORY: THE GREAT CHAIN

America's fight for independence had begun. The Revolutionary War would be primarily fought in towns, villages, and seaports along the New England coast, with one of Britain's main objectives being to control the city of Boston.

The wide Hudson River that flowed from Canada to New York City, and eventually into the Atlantic Ocean, functioned as a demarcation line between New England and the western colonies. It was obvious that to conquer New England, the British would need to float their fleet up the river to attack from the west while the Atlantic fleet attacked from the east. The British already controlled both ends of the river in Canada and New York City.

The patriots also recognized the strategic importance of the Hudson, and that it would be key to either their victory or defeat. With that in mind, they came up with a brilliant plan to stop the British from freely traveling the river: They would construct a blockade—but not just any blockade. A massive steel one.

The blocking of rivers during times of war was nothing new. Over the centuries, logs, rocks, and even sunken ships were used to prevent opposing forces to gain access to a river or bay. But this blockade would be different. After being contacted by General George Washington, experienced engineer and canal builder Thomas Machin was tasked with the job of creating this new blockade, and what a formidable task it would be. The Hudson River was up to a mile wide in many areas, extremely deep, and had a very swift current. It would be impossible to block the river using the standard methods of the day.

Machin's answer was to create an 1,800-foot steel chain that would stretch across the river on log rafts. The links of the chain were forged in secret at furnaces across the region and then floated by raft up the Hudson River to an area called West Point. At the time, West Point was no more than an earth-and-wood redoubt, not the spectacular military academy it is today, but it was the narrowest section of the river. Each link of the chain ranged in length from 19 to 36 inches long and weighed up to 80 pounds. The entire length of chain when assembled would weigh 80 tons. The ends would be anchored into the rocky banks on each side of the river and the chain floated across on wooden rafts. The center of the chain could be detached so that friendly vessels could pass. The chain could also be detached from its anchor points on the banks and stored away during the winter months when the river would freeze.

The plan worked. The chain was so ominous that British ships never tempted fate and tried to cross it. Today, thirteen links from that same chain can still be seen at West Point's Trophy Point, where the western side of the blockade was anchored, along with a plaque commemorating this unique piece of Revolutionary War history.

· 4 ·

PRINCESS CHARLOTTE AND THE GREAT RUSSIAN ROYALTY HOAX

We take one more trip to the Gulf Coast and the New World, specifically, French Louisiana, for a tale of romance and deceit in the early 1700s. One more time we visit the town of Mobile for a story that has been passed down over the centuries by several nineteenth-century regional historians, including François Xavier Martin, Albert Pickett, and Charles Gayarré. The tale was so powerful that in 1804, it was made into a novella by German-Swiss author Johann Heinrich Daniel Zschokke, *Die Prinzessin von Wolfenbüttel*, recognized as the first German romance novel. Duke Ernest of Saxe-Coburg also told a version of the story, this one as an opera, *Santa Chiara*, only this telling occurred in Russia and Italy and not the early settlement of Mobile.

It is a riveting tale of romance and deception, but is it true? Did a real Russian princess fake her death and come to the ramshackle Fort Louis de la Mobile to escape? Was it simply a hoax perpetrated on the people there? Some regional historians, including Jay Higginbotham, believe this is the case. Parts of the story may be true while others could simply be how the story has morphed over the years into the tale we know today. While we may never know the truth, it is a wonderful tale with international flair that is well worth retelling.

The story revolves around the life of Charlotte Christine Sophia of Brunswick-Wolfenbüttel, the daughter of the Duke of Brunswick-Wolfenbüttel, Louis Rudolph, and Princess Christine Louise of Oettingen-Oettingen. Charlotte was raised in the court of Polish king August II, where she received an excellent education, and where she met Alexi Petrovich, the son of Russian tsar, Peter the Great, who had sent his son to the court to finish his own education in 1709.

The couple met and fell in love. Peter approved of the relationship because he believed it would be to his advantage. Charlotte's sister, Elisabeth Christine, had married Karl IV of Austria, the Holy Roman Emperor. Peter thought that if Charlotte and Alexi would marry, he would have the perfect ally in the Holy Roman Emperor, if and when he went to war with the Turks, which he eventually did.

Charlotte and Alexi were married in 1711 in Torgau, Germany, thus making Charlotte the first European woman to marry into Russian royalty. What began as a happy marriage quickly devolved into an abusive relationship. Peter would often take his son away for extended periods of time to fight in Russia's twenty-one-year-long war with Sweden, known as the Great Northern War. When Alexi returned home from these junkets, Charlotte was surprised to find that he had turned into a violent drunk. On top of that, Alexi was having an unconcealed affair with a Russian serf, Yefrosinya ("Afrosinya") Fedorova, who belonged to Alexi's tutor. Charlotte felt alone and isolated to the point where she left Alexi and fled back to her family in Germany, but Peter would have nothing of that, and returned her to Russia.

Charlotte and Alexi had two children. The first was daughter Natalia, who died at an early age from tuberculosis. Not long after, their son, Peter II, was born, but he also died at a young age. Official records tell us that Charlotte herself died one month after the birth of her son.

That's the end of the story, right? Not quite. Here's where things get murky. As the story goes, despondent over her cruel marriage and the deep desire to leave Russia and her husband behind, just prior to her death, Charlotte had made a request of Peter, Alexi, and her servants. If she were to die, she did not want her body embalmed. Soon after, in 1715, she drank a liquid that made it appear that she was dead. This is where things take a sharp turn at a fork in the road.

One account, the *Santa Chiara* opera version, says that instead of being placed in a coffin, Charlotte had a wooden doll placed there by her servants, and when she awoke from the drink she had ingested, she fled the country. Another account says that her body was actually placed in the coffin and moved to the royal mausoleum. Several hours later, after everyone had left the mausoleum, the servants entered the tomb, opened the coffin, and freed the now very much awake and very much alive princess, and she fled the country.

Our tale now takes us to the French colony of Mobile. The original Fort Louis de la Mobile had been moved approximately 20 miles south from its previous location on the banks of the Mobile River to a location much closer to the Gulf of Mexico, along the banks of Mobile Bay, in 1711. Ten years after the move, a new fort made with bricks, stone, and an earthen breastwork was built, named Fort Conde. Despite the move, the settlement was still facing the same hardships the previous fort upriver was facing: food shortages, devastating hurricanes, mosquitoes, and yellow fever. It was certainly not a place where one would expect anyone of importance, especially royalty, to arrive and begin a new life, but, according to the five hundred residents of the fort and surrounding villages, it did happen.

It was the summer of 1721 when a German "pest ship" arrived at the fort. These ships set sail from Europe to the new colonies on the Gulf Coast in hopes of a better life. Many of the passengers died on these voyages due to the pestilence that ran rampant throughout the vessel, giving them their unfortunate moniker. When this particular ship arrived at Fort Conde, two hundred German immigrants disembarked, all determined to head inland to begin a new life.

One of the passengers that stepped off the boat stood out from the rest. Those in attendance described this passenger as being the most beautiful woman they had ever seen. She was dressed immaculately in fine, expensive clothing. Her body was adorned with exquisite jewelry. Local historian Caldwell Delaney wrote that the young woman was "not of the common herd." A rumor began circulating among the colonists that this young woman was none other than Princess Charlotte Christine Sophia of Brunswick-Wolfenbüttel, the wife of Peter the Great's son.

When pressed by onlookers about her identity, the young woman would only say that she was not at liberty to discuss the matter because she was traveling incognito, which only added fuel to the mystery, feeding the rumor she was indeed Charlotte, and fleeing her cheating, drunken, and abusive husband.

Not everyone at the fort was convinced that this person was the princess. Several military officials stationed at the fort had heard that the princess had died six years earlier, in 1715, and that she had been buried in St. Petersburg, Russia. One young officer at the fort, Chevalier d'Aubert, came forward and made a proclamation that he recognized the woman. He had had the chance to meet the princess some years ago, and this woman, he said, was indeed Princess Charlotte.

Charlotte settled down in a little cottage near the fort and made herself at home in the village. Chevalier d'Aubert would often come calling, and eventually, the two fell in love and were married. Soon after, the couple welcomed a baby girl into their home.

Years later, d'Aubert left his wife and daughter behind when he was reassigned from Fort Louis de la Mobile and sent north some 200 miles as the crow flies to the French settlement of Fort Toulouse, only a few miles north of present-day Montgomery. One year later, feeling alone and longing for her husband, Charlotte packed up their baby and along with a female servant, climbed onto a boat that would take them up the winding Mobile and Alabama Rivers, so meandering that the journey would take fifty days to complete.

Upon their arrival at the fort, d'Aubert was thrilled to see his family. Charlotte was welcomed with open arms by both the residents of Fort Toulouse and local Native American tribes who frequented and traded with the fort. Chevalier d'Aubert did not want his family to live in the shabby conditions inside the fort, so he set about building a special cabin just for Charlotte, the baby, and himself. As historian Caldwell Delaney put it, "It was a far cry from the Imperial Palace of St. Petersburg, but it was happiness and content."

Eventually, d'Aubert was called back to France, and this time, he brought his wife and daughter with him. Chevalier d'Aubert passed away in 1754, leaving Charlotte alone once again.

But the story doesn't end there. One day, a German nobleman, the Count of Saxony, spotted the young woman strolling through the Tuileries Garden in Paris. He immediately recognized the woman. This was not Princess Charlotte, but one of Charlotte's former wardrobe servants. The count reported the sighting and revealed the woman's identity to writer François-Marie Arouet (better known as Voltaire), who wrote up the story for the local press.

Apparently, Charlotte *had* died in 1715, and her servant had absconded with some of the princess's clothing and jewelry, climbed aboard that German ship, and sailed to Mobile. Her incredible likeness to Charlotte made most of the residents at Fort Conde believe she was actually the princess. With her cover blown, this unnamed wardrobe servant quietly disappeared and died penniless, leaving behind a fascinating story that still resonates to this day along the US Gulf Coast.

FOOTNOTE TO HISTORY: DOLLAR PRINCESSES

The British aristocracy had one thing that young, wealthy American women wanted. It wasn't their money. It was a title, and the British gentry were more than willing to oblige.

Beginning around 1874, England was facing an economic crisis. The United States had found its footing and had become a major international agricultural center, exporting its grain and other commodities to buyers around the world. This put the British gentry in a bind: All of their wealth was tied up in agricultural land and grain sales, and now the United States was outpacing them in agricultural production and trade. Combine this with the rapid rise of industrialization in the United States, and the British aristocracy was now facing tough times financially. They owned large and opulent mansions but couldn't afford to run or maintain them. They were basically second-class citizens compared to their wealthy American cousins.

At the same time, this newfound wealth in America saw the incredibly rapid growth of

America's upper class. This period in American history became known as the Gilded Age, a time when wealth and status meant everything. The daughters of these rich families became heiresses to enormous fortunes. Wealth wasn't all the parents of these heiresses wanted for their daughters, however; they also wanted the status that went along with holding a title.

So, these young American heiresses were looking for a bit of status—a British title would do nicely, thank you—while British noblemen were looking for cash. It was the perfect combination, and the concept of the "dollar princess" was born.

Basically, wealthy American mothers and daughters would fly to London during what was called the "social season," and with the aid of a guidebook, they would begin their quest. The guidebook was basically an advertisement that provided a list of recent matches, sort of a "here's what we can do for you" advertisement, as well as a list of eligible single dukes, earls, and barons who were just waiting for an invitation from one of these heiresses to meet. After a brief meeting and courtship, a wedding was arranged. Sometimes, if the couple was lucky, there was actually a love connection between them, but just as many marriages were merely contractual: She got the title, he got the money.

One of the most famous and earliest examples of one of these unions was the marriage between Jennie Jerome and Lord Randolph Churchill. Jerome was the daughter of Wall Street tycoon, Leonard Jerome. You would think that would be enough to get the family into New York's high society, but rumors that her mother was part Iroquois left the family shunned by the city's elite. The solution was to go to England to meet an eligible bachelor nobleman. Lord Churchill was the youngest son of the seventh duke of Marlboro. When the two met, it was love at first sight, and within three days of their meeting, they were married. Suddenly, Jennie's family was recognized by the well-to-do in the city.

Jennie and Randolph would eventually make history with the birth of their son, Winston, who would later become prime minister of Britain and lead that country to victory in World War II.

· 5 ·

AMERICA'S FIRST BLACK
WOMAN POLITICAL WRITER
AND ABOLITIONIST,
MARIA W. STEWART

The Boston-based publisher William Lloyd Garrison was in for a surprise when a twenty-nine-year-old Black woman walked into his office one morning in 1831. The office was the home of *The Liberator*, a newly established four-page radical abolitionist weekly newspaper. The newspaper's mission was to advocate for an immediate end to slavery and called for the immediate integration of previously enslaved people into American society.

To Garrison, Maria W. Stewart appeared to be destitute and illiterate, but his first impression morphed into one of amazement when she handed him a manuscript. The publisher later wrote of the moment in a letter to her:

> [You] placed in my hands, for criticism and friendly advice, a manuscript Embodying your devotional thoughts and aspirations, and also various essays pertaining to the conditions of that class with which you were complexionally identified—a class "peeled, meted out, and

trodden underfoot." . . . *I was impressed with your intelligence and excellence of character.*

Garrison would publish that manuscript, which Stewart called a "meditation," and from that moment until her death in 1879, Maria W. Stewart became a prolific political writer, a champion for the abolition of slavery, and a woman's rights advocate—or, as historians have dubbed her, America's first Black woman political writer.

Maria Miller was born in 1803, in Hartford, Connecticut. By the age of five, this daughter of two African-born parents was orphaned and had been "bonded out" as an indentured servant to a minister. At sixteen, the young woman moved to Boston's Beacon Hill district, an area where the upper class lived in the southern and eastern sections of the city, while working, middle-class people of all races, including free African Americans, lived in the northern and western sections. The latter section of Beacon Hill would become a hotbed of abolitionists and Underground Railroad activity leading up to the Civil War.

Upon her arrival, Maria gained work as a domestic servant while at the same time attending Sunday Sabbath School, offered by a local Seventh-day Adventist Church. It was here that Maria met her future husband, James Stewart, who was a War of 1812 veteran and successful shipping agent. Stewart was forty-seven years old, twenty-four years older than Maria. The couple married in 1826.

Her husband's standing in the vibrant free Black community of Beacon Hill offered Maria the chance to continue her education, mostly self-taught, and to make important connections that would help to shape her political and social views of the world. One of the most notable was David Walker, a radical abolitionist who called for Blacks of all standing to rise up and fight against oppression and enslavement. Walker was a huge proponent of Black nationalism—the creation of a separate Black nation. His pamphlet, "David Walker's Appeal to Coloured Citizens of the World," was extremely influential to many free Blacks, including Maria.

In 1829, James Stewart died from heart disease. Although he had left his grieving wife well off financially, due to the unscrupulous behavior of White businessmen and bankers, Maria was denied her inheritance, leaving her once again to fend for herself. Three months after her husband's passing, her good friend and mentor, David Walker, also passed away.

Following these dual tragic losses in her life, Maria clung to her faith, while at the same time, feeling increasingly liberated to speak out about issues concerning Blacks in America. This is when she set pen to paper and authored the essay "Religion and the Pure Principles of Morality, the Sure Foundation on Which We Must Build." Using biblical scripture and images, a formula that she would use in her future writings, Maria condemned slavery and White oppression, and called for Blacks to fight for their rights, even if force were required.

This was the essay she delivered to *The Liberator*'s office in January 1831, published a short time thereafter to high acclaim. Following its publication, Maria would author more essays for the newspaper. Soon, she was asked to take her message to the public and address various groups in person, around Boston. Between the time the first essay was published and 1833, Maria gave four public presentations, promoting her views on all matters, not only to Blacks, but to White audiences as well, or at least those who would hear her out.

Her first speech came in April 1832 at a meeting of the women's African-American Female Intelligence Society, an organization comprised solely of women, and created by free Black women of Boston. Soon after, Maria made history when she was asked to address an audience comprising both men and women at Boston's Franklin Hall, something unheard of for the time. It was considered "unseemly" for a woman to speak publicly, especially about politics, and it was even more contrary to beliefs in that era for a woman to address a group of men, let alone that it was a Black woman who would be doing the presentation.

The address in Franklin Hall, the site of many antislavery meetings held in the New England area, was delivered on September 21, 1832, and would mark the first time in American history that a woman, Black or White, would address an audience of both men and women publicly on political issues. But it wouldn't be the last. In her speeches, Maria used a gospel speaking style to motivate and inspire her audiences and used biblical references to make her points. She empowered women to seek strength through education and to use that strength to gain a foothold in the business world. She called for Black unity and pride and continued her quest for the abolition of slavery.

In the 1832 address at Franklin Hall, Maria focused primarily on Black women, calling on them to rise up and acquire an education; she condemned the attitude of the world around them that denied women this education, and in turn, the opportunity to advance with better employment. The speech not only called for women to rise up, but also called for equal rights for all Blacks in the Northern industrial states. She also questioned the motivation and thinking behind Black nationalism, a plan her dear friend David Walker had once espoused. Her speech began with a question:

> Why ye sit here and die? If we say we go to a foreign land, the famine and the pestilence is there. If we sit here, we shall die. Come, let us plead our case before the whites: if they save us alive, and if they kill us, we shall die. Methinks I heard a spiritual interrogation: "Who

shall go forward and take off the reproach that is cast upon the people of color? Shall it be a woman?" And my heart made this reply: "If it is thy will, be it even so, Lord Jesus!"

The entirety of her first two speeches were printed in *The Liberator*, the second one appearing in the newspaper under an illustration of a woman shackled in chains, asking, "Am I not a woman and a sister?" Maria Stewart quickly rose to fame in and around the Boston area, where she was either hailed for her candor on such pressing subjects or attacked as being a radical orator. Maria was busting through long-held social norms, completely taboo for the time.

After a second pamphlet of Stewart's essays was published by Garrison, "Meditations from the Pen of Mrs. Maria W. Stewart," Maria would give two more public lectures. The third came on February 23, 1833, at Boston's African Masonic Hall, and was titled, "African Rights and Liberty." It was during this speech that Stewart came to the realization that even with the success she was having, enlightening Boston's free Blacks, she was also being met with increasingly violent resistance. At one of the speeches, the Black men in the audience jeered and threw rotten tomatoes at her. By now, even her friends in Boston were beginning to turn on the social advocate because she was upsetting the status quo.

Stewart began to fear for her life, to the point where, just two short years after the publication of her first essay, she decided it was time to leave Boston. In all, Maria Stewart gave only four public speeches. Her final speech in Boston before moving to New York City came on September 21, 1833. In what is known as her "Farewell Speech," Maria addressed the backlash she was receiving from her friends and the Black community in general:

During this short period of my Christian warfare, I have indeed had to contend against the fiery darts of the devil. And was it not that the righteous are kept by the mighty power of God through faith unto salvation, long before this I should have proved to like the seed by the wayside; for it has actually appeared to me, at different periods, as though the powers of earth and hell had combined against me, to prove my overthrow. . . . The bitterness of my soul has departed from those who endeavored to discourage and hinder me in my Christian progress, and I can now forgive my enemies, bless those who have hated me, and cheerfully pray for those who have spitefully used and persecuted me.

Though dismayed over the attacks she was enduring for her outspoken stances, Stewart never gave up the fight. After moving to New York, she earned a living by becoming a public school teacher in Manhattan. Maria would attend many antislavery conventions in the city, even befriending famed abolitionist Frederick Douglass. She continued writing essays, although she never spoke publicly again.

Maria would eventually move to Baltimore around 1852, and then to Washington, DC, when the Civil War began. Here, she continued teaching, and took a position as head of housekeeping at the Freedmen's Hospital and Asylum, a position once held by abolitionist Sojourner Truth.

In 1878, a new law was passed that finally allowed widows of War of 1812 veterans to receive financial assistance. Petitioning the government, Maria began receiving her husband's pension of eight dollars a month. With that money, she published an updated version of "Meditations from the Pen of Mrs. Maria W. Stewart" that included several new essays. One year later, Maria Stewart passed away.

While not as famous as Frederick Douglass or Sojourner Truth, the work of Maria Stewart is just as important and needs to be heralded today.

FOOTNOTE TO HISTORY:
THE FIRST ABOLITIONIST, BENJAMIN LAY

In 2018, regional groups of the Religious Society of Friends, better known as the Quakers, were holding their annual meetings across the country. During those meetings, a joint statement was read to the congregations: "We hold that Benjamin Lay was a friend of the truth. We are in unity with the spirit of Benjamin Lay."

Over 250 years prior, a biographer and one of the signers of the Declaration of Independence, Benjamin Rush, commented on this fellow that the Quakers were standing in unity with, saying, "There was a time when the name of this celebrated Christian philosopher [Benjamin Lay] was familiar to every man, woman, and to nearly every child in Pennsylvania."

Who was this celebrated Benjamin Lay, and what role did he play in American history? His philosophies were unique, to say the least, even radical in the British colonies of North America in the early eighteenth century. They were even radical for his Quaker faith.

Benjamin Lay was a hunchbacked little person, standing at just four feet tall. If we didn't know the time period of his life, a simple description of him would make you think we were talking about a 1960s flower child. His philosophy was naturalistic. He believed in a simpler world, choosing to live in a cave in the hills of Pennsylvania. He believed that people should respect nature, living only on fruits and vegetables they grew themselves, as he called it, "the innocent fruits of the earth," and should make their own clothes. He advocated for animal rights, and held an opinion that was contrary to that of most people during the early 1700s: Slavery had to be abolished.

His antislavery sentiments grew after a trip to Barbados where he witnessed the slave trade firsthand. When he returned to the colonies, he began advocating for the abolition of slavery, but his methods were a bit too radical for his Quaker religion. When Lay was invited to a dinner party, if the food had been grown and harvested by slave labor, or if he found out the host was a slave owner, he would throw the food away and storm out. His beliefs on slavery angered the Quakers even more when he published a book in 1737 titled *All Slave Keepers that Keep the Innocent in Bondage, Apostates*. The book chastised his Quaker Friends for what he believed were actions contrary to the religion's teachings. He even went so far as to name names.

His most famous protest came during the Quakers' Philadelphia Yearly Meeting in September 1738. Walking 20 miles from his cave and wearing an oversized coat, when it was his turn to speak, Lay ripped off the coat to reveal that he was wearing a military uniform complete with sword underneath, a blasphemous statement in and of itself in the Quaker religion, which promoted peacemaking. In a secret compartment stitched into the uniform, Lay had hidden a pig's bladder filled with red pokeberry juice.

Holding the sword high above his head, he shouted, "Thus shall God shed the blood of those persons who enslave their fellow creatures," then plunged the sword into the bladder. The "blood" gushed out. Some of the members of the congregation passed out from shock. Lay then splattered anyone in the room who was a slaveholder with the symbolic blood.

Lay was removed from the meeting and disowned by the Quakers. Despite being shunned by his religion, Lay continued to profess his beliefs in equality for all humans, no matter their status or the color of their skin.

In 2015, historian Marcus Rediker wrote a biography on Lay which came to the attention of the Abington (Pennsylvania) Friends Meeting, where Lay had held his dramatic protest. The members were unaware of Lay's story, and as a result of the book, the annual Quaker meetings in 2018 finally recognized Benjamin Lay, America's first abolitionist.

· 6 ·

LAURA SECORD: WAR OF 1812 CANADIAN HEROINE

Historians call the War of 1812 America's first forgotten war. Sandwiched between the American Revolution and the Civil War, the second war between Britain and the United States barely receives a mention in public school history classes anymore. Nonetheless, the end result of the conflict was of extreme importance to the fledgling country in that it achieved international recognition as an emerging and powerful trading partner. The Americans now saw themselves not as citizens of separate states, but rather as part of a unified nation, a group of *united* states.

As with any war, whether history remembers it or not, there were a few names from the War of 1812 that gained prominence years later, including that of General Andrew Jackson, who later became the country's seventh president. Many others also played a role in the war, even though their names have been virtually lost to history, and one of those is a young woman who became a Canadian heroine of the war, Laura Ingersoll Secord.

Now, you may have noticed the title of this chapter indicates that Laura was a "Canadian heroine," even though this book is subtitled "21 Extraordinary Stories from Forgotten *American*

History." The reason will become evident in a moment, but truth be known, Laura was an American.

The story begins with Thomas Ingersoll, a successful hat-maker, who married seventeen-year-old Elizabeth Dewey on February 28, 1775, in Great Barrington, a small town in the colony of Massachusetts. His success in business afforded the newlyweds the opportunity to purchase a parcel of land of their own in town. They built a large house complete with servants' quarters attached to the back of the building, and Thomas's shop off to the right side of the structure.

Two months after their marriage, history would be forever changed as the American Revolution began. Much like the Civil War almost one hundred years later, families and friends were ripped apart. You were either a loyalist to the monarchy or a patriot. There was no gray area. Patriots would often take matters into their own hands and violently turn on anyone who was a loyalist, often destroying their homes and businesses, sometimes resorting to tarring and feathering British loyalists. As a result, many loyalists were driven from their homes and forced to flee to England.

It was during this time of violence and revolt that Laura Ingersoll, the first child of Thomas and Elizabeth, was born, on September 13, 1775. As the war waged on around them, Laura's father took up arms, siding with the patriots and joining the state militia to fight the war. When the militia merged into the new Continental Army, Thomas quickly rose in the ranks, from second lieutenant to captain. All of this meant that Thomas Ingersoll was frequently away from home, but even still, over the next nine years, Thomas and Elizabeth would grow their family. Their second child, Elizabeth Franks, was born in 1779, followed by Mira in 1781, and Abigail in 1783. With her father often heading off to battle, Laura became extremely close to her mother, taking on the role of surrogate parent to help her mother with caring for her siblings.

The war finally ended in 1783 when the Treaty of Paris was signed between Britain, France, and the United States. Thomas was appointed magistrate of Great Barrington. One year later, tragedy struck the Ingersoll household when Laura's mother suddenly passed away. Thomas didn't feel he could take care of the youngest child, Abigail, who was still an infant, so he decided it would be best for Abigail to be adopted. Laura would continue to help take care of her other siblings, even though she was only eight years old.

Just over one year later, Thomas married Mercy Smith, the woman who would teach Laura how to read, and about art. Tragically, Mercy passed away due to tuberculosis not soon after. Four months after her death, Thomas would marry once again, this time to Sarah Backus, a war widow, who had one daughter, ten-year-old Harriet. Over the years, Thomas and Sarah would have seven more children, and at sixteen, Laura was happily taking on the responsibility of watching over them, along with her stepmother. But the family wasn't finished growing. Two more children were born, one in 1793 and another in 1794.

By now, the newly formed United States was trying to survive a depression. Their money was worthless. Feed, grain, and meat were often used as payment for goods and services. Even though a treaty had been signed, Britain was still making life difficult for businessmen in the United States by dumping goods on the new country while at the same time limiting what and how much Americans could sell in Britain.

With money being extremely tight, especially for a burgeoning family, and the continued harassment and violence against any remaining loyalists in the country, Thomas petitioned the Canadian government for a plot of land near Niagara, in Queenston, Ontario. When his petition was granted, he packed up the family and began the journey to their new home.

Getting to the property was a harrowing journey, to say the least. All eleven children and their belongings were loaded onto a wagon and driven to the Hudson River, where they boarded a small boat and headed upstream to the town of Schenectady, where another wagon took them to the Mohawk River. There, they climbed aboard a large flat-bottomed vessel known as a Durham boat for the next leg of the journey. The boat was powered by four crew members who either paddled when the boat was in deeper water or used "setting poles" to push the raft forward in the shallows.

The family had to portage in areas where the river became too shallow, in all, walking 30 miles of portages before reaching Oswego River and the final leg of the journey. As they were crossing the lake, a violent storm moved in. The boat they were on was tossed about like a toy. Several times it nearly capsized as passengers screamed in horror. The storm caused days of delay, so much so that the passengers nearly ran out of food.

Finally, the Ingersoll family arrived at their destination, Queenston, the perfect spot for a businessman to set up shop. Located on the banks of the Niagara River, the town was an important stop for passengers, and for merchant vessels, to disembark and unload cargo before making their way around the raging rapids and falls ahead.

Thomas reinvented himself and opened the Ingersoll Tavern here, although it was not in business for long. There was a fear that another war was imminent in North America as France and Britain went to war once again in Europe. The settlement of Queenston was moved and a new settlement was established farther north, near the town of York. Thomas took over a previously established tavern in town called the Government House.

His oldest daughter, Laura, didn't make the move north. She had met the son of one of the most prosperous families in the area, James Secord. The year was 1796 when the twenty-one-year-old Laura, described as a belle of the region's social scene, met James when he visited her father's tavern. He immediately fell in love with her, and they were married in June the following year. Three years later, she would give birth to the couple's first child, Mary.

As the 1800s rolled around, France and Britain were waging war against one another again in Europe. The United States attempted to remain neutral in the conflict and was enjoying free trade between the two warring nations. Napoleon's Berlin Decree of 1806 declared that any neutral ship that visited a British-held port was an enemy of France. One year later, Britain retaliated with their own order, the Order in Council, which required that a neutral country obtain a license before trading with France. In response to that order, France authorized the capture of any ship from a neutral country, which in turn gave Britain the green light to seize neutral ships as well, taking their cargo and capturing the crew and putting them into service with the Royal Navy.

In 1809, the US Congress passed the Non-Intercourse Act, which prevented all trade with Britain and France. Meanwhile, tensions were mounting in the western region of the new country, where Native American tribes were taking notice of the Americans' encroachment on their land. And to the north, Canadians were eyeing American aggression against the Indians as a sign that the United States was beginning a war of conquest to expand its territory.

Complicated, right? All of this back-and-forth eventually led to the United States declaring war on Britain on June 18, 1812, and the War of 1812 began.

The British army stationed in Queenston and under the command of General Isaac Brock feared that American troops would attempt to invade Canada and take control of the entire region known as Upper Canada. If that happened, the entire province would be in danger of American occupation.

Brock was correct about the invasion, just not the location where American troops would cross the swift waters of the

Niagara River to begin the attack. On October 12, 1812, General Stephen Van Rensselaer led the New York militia across the river and stormed a hillside where they captured a V-shaped structure called a redan, lined with British cannons. It looked as if the Americans might just take control of the Canadian province.

General Brock, awakened by the sound of gunfire, hopped on his horse, gathered his troops, and rode in to do battle with the Americans. With sword drawn, Brock was killed by a single sniper bullet. It would take a group of First Nation tribes—Mohawk, Haudenosaunee, and Delaware Indians—to trap the Americans on the hills surrounding Queenston, keeping them pinned down long enough for British reinforcements to arrive.

Cannon fire echoed through Queenston, shaking Laura Secord and her own growing family awake. Laura gathered her children and ran out the back door. Years later, Laura recalled the family fleeing for their lives with "cannonballs flying around [us] in every direction."

Laura and the children ran a mile to a farmhouse where other families of the village had gathered. Her children were safe, but she worried about her husband, James, who had become a sergeant in the local militia and was fighting in the Battle of Queenston Heights. Late in the day, as a lull in the fighting settled over the valley, Laura made a decision: She left her children in the care of her eldest daughter, huddled together in the farmhouse with the other families, and she raced back home to see if her husband was there.

When she arrived, a wounded messenger met her with the news that James had been wounded and was lying on the battlefield. What happened next is best described by author Peggy Dymond Leavey in her book, *Laura Secord: Heroine of the War of 1812*:

> *[Laura] lifted her skirts and climbed the steep hill to the scene of the battle. At the sight of the dead from both sides of the battle and the*

moans of the injured dying amongst them, Laura was filled with
horror. She picked her way through all the red and blue uniformed
figures on the ground until at last she found her husband.

James lay there in great pain, weak from a tremendous loss of blood. Tearing off a piece of her dress, she fashioned a compress to stem the bleeding. An officer saw what she was doing and helped her bring James back down the hill to their house, which had been completely vandalized by American soldiers. But that didn't matter to Laura. She had saved her husband's life.

By day's end, with one last enormous volley of gunfire, the Battle of Queenston Heights ended as the American troops surrendered. In the end, 1,000 Americans were captured and 300 were killed or wounded, while only 28 British soldiers were wounded or killed. With their house having been virtually destroyed by the Americans, and with James in need of medical attention, Laura and James packed up what little possessions remained and moved the family to St. David's, just outside of the town of Niagara.

On May 25, 1813, American cannons roared once again from positions across the Niagara River, from Fort George. The cannons kept up a sustained bombardment, engulfing the wooden fort in fire.

Two days after the bombardment, American troops paddled across the river and successfully took control of the fort and the town of Niagara. The British army was forced to retreat. Under the command of Lieutenant James FitzGibbon, the troops moved 30 miles north to Beaver Dams, where they set up camp at a cabin owned by British loyalist John DeCew.

Back in the towns around Niagara, the Americans quickly moved in and made themselves at home. Residents in the area were forced into providing American soldiers with housing and meals during their occupation. This is when Laura's incredible story went to a new level.

One evening, Laura overheard a conversation between some of the soldiers who were billeting in her home. What she heard stunned her: The Americans were planning a major attack on British troops at Beaver Dams. Laura shared this news with her husband, who was still recuperating from his injury. She told him that someone needed to warn the colonel.

"Well," he replied, "if I crawled there on my hand and knees, I could not get there in time."

Laura suggested that she go instead.

"You go?" he said. "I do not think any man could get through, let alone a woman."

In 1853, Laura recalled the event in a memoir, writing that she needed to "put the British troops under FitzGibbon in possession of [the plan] and if possible, to save the British troops from capture or perhaps total destruction."

On the morning of June 22, Laura dressed in a brown cotton housedress, a muslin kerchief, and leather slippers and headed out into the darkness to begin her journey, a trek of more than 20 miles. Before embarking on the most difficult part of the journey, Laura visited with her in-law Hannah Secord and her daughter Elizabeth. When she told the women what her plan was, she was shocked when Elizabeth volunteered to go with her.

From there, the route to Beaver Dams was perilous. They would have to cross through an area called Black Swamp, a dark and dismal mosquito- and snake-infested bog that offered no firm footing. Its spongy moss covered the banks, and the thick muck made it extremely difficult to navigate. As the sun rose, so did the summer heat. By now, Elizabeth was near exhaustion, so Laura led her to a family friend's house in nearby Shipman's Corners where she could recuperate while Laura continued on.

Walking through dense, unmarked forest and using the banks of Twelve Mile Creek as a guide to her destination, the risk of a wild animal attack was ever present. That, and the fear of human contact from both hostile American soldiers and unfriendly Indians. Her slippers were lost when she crossed the swamp, leaving her feet severely blistered, and her body was ravaged with cuts and bruises, but Laura finally emerged from the forest—and immediately found herself surrounded by tribesmen. Without fear, she addressed the chief and told him that she had urgent information for FitzGibbon. Reluctantly, the chief agreed to let her pass, and with a few warriors helping to guide her, she arrived at the cabin where the colonel was staying, a 20-mile trek that took seventeen hours.

After telling the colonel what she knew and undergoing a short interrogation to verify she wasn't an American spy, Laura collapsed with exhaustion. The following morning, an Indian scout reported to FitzGibbon that American troops were on the move. The young woman's intelligence was correct, and the colonel went into action.

After a short delay, the Americans continued their march on Beaver Dams, but when they arrived, they were ambushed by a large contingent of Indigenous warriors. The Americans, having heard mostly unfounded stories about the savagery of these tribes, turned and ran, only to be forced to surrender by approaching British forces led by FitzGibbon.

Laura Secord was a true Canadian hero of the War of 1812. Sadly, very few have heard her story. In fact, Secord and the Iroquois warriors who actually won the Battle of Beaver Dams were relegated to the dustbin of history. FitzGibbon was applauded for "his" victory. Laura petitioned the government several times to receive a commission in honor of her efforts but was refused, even when FitzGibbon wrote letters of recommendation for her, acknowledging that she was the one that had alerted him to act, but the petitions were ignored.

Laura's husband James died in 1841, ending his military pension and leaving Laura in poverty. It wasn't until 1860 that the story of Laura Secord's heroics was finally revealed, and the Prince of Wales awarded her £100 for her actions.

Laura Secord died in 1868 and was buried in Drummond Hill Cemetery in Niagara Falls, where an 8-foot-tall marble tombstone commemorates the heroine of the War of 1812.

FOOTNOTE TO HISTORY: THE UNITED STATES OF NEW ENGLAND

The War of 1812 started during a complicated time in world history. In Europe, wars were raging between France and Britain as the two countries vied for supremacy over the Continent. Meanwhile, the United States was merrily trading with both countries, making every effort to be neutral. Britain felt the United States had broken the Jay Treaty that they had jointly signed in 1794, saying that Americans were playing both sides of the fence. British warships began harassing and threatening US merchant ships on the high seas. Ships of the Royal Navy would engage US merchant vessels and, in many cases, capture the sailors on board, impressing them into service for Britain.

In 1807, President Thomas Jefferson attempted to end the harassment by invoking the Embargo Act, a policy whereby US merchant vessels were forbidden from doing any business with any country. The effect of being forced to end trade with both France and Britain, two of the most powerful nations in the world, was devastating on the economy of the New England states, whose prime economic driver was shipping. Their economy went into free fall, and as historian and author James Ellis points out, over half of the workforce in New England suddenly found themselves out of work.

When James Madison took over the presidency in 1809, he established further, and harsher, economic sanctions against Britain, and when the War of 1812 finally exploded between the two countries on June 18, 1812, New Englanders, already reeling from the sanctions imposed by Washington, did not fully support the war. Instead, they favored peace between the two nations and wanted the two to become stronger trading partners.

Seeing this as their opportunity, on December 15, 1814, members of the Rhode Island, Connecticut, Vermont, and New Hampshire Federalist Party met in secret in Hartford, Connecticut, to discuss their options. The men met for three weeks in what became known as the Hartford Convention. During the meetings, several resolutions were bandied about, ranging from simply issuing a public criticism of President Madison to the more extreme position of seceding from the Union. Moderate members at the convention were concerned that even the suggestion of splitting from the United States to form their own union would cause a civil war in the country.

In the end, cooler heads prevailed, and a series of resolutions were adopted that formed the basis for states' rights, including calling on the United States to end its policy of conscription (pulling state militia members into federal military service). It also demanded that a two-thirds majority vote in Congress be required before a president could send the country to war and requested aid from the federal government to bolster the crashing New England economy.

As it turned out, it was too little, too late. As the convention concluded, the Treaty of Ghent was signed and the war was over. Trade relations with Britain resumed, and New England began to thrive once again.

The resolutions that were discussed during the Hartford Convention were eventually read into the congressional record in Washington, on both the House and Senate floors, and a few of the recommendations—most importantly, the two-thirds vote required to go to war—were adopted.

· 7 ·

THE TWO-GIRL ARMY

Over the course of history, there have been countless battles fought in the heat of war. But for as many bloody conflicts that have taken place, there have also been countless times when conflicts have been averted, either through peaceful negotiations, or when cooler heads prevailed, as we saw earlier with the Pig War of 1859. On very rare occasions, there have been times when all-out warfare and bloodshed have been averted through the efforts of average folks who took a chance and put their own lives in peril, saving the lives of countless others by their actions. These are David vs. Goliath stories, ordinary people taking on a seemingly insurmountable force and coming out the victor.

This is one of those incredible tales whose veracity has been disputed over the years. While some of the details have become blurry over the centuries, research by historians lands squarely on the fact that it did happen. It is a tale of two young girls whose quick thinking saved their town from devastation and turned back the mighty British navy during the War of 1812.

The story takes place in Scituate Harbor, Massachusetts, a quintessential New England fishing village that over the years has turned into a popular tourist destination. Picturesque historic homes line the rocky shores; visitors stroll along sprawling beaches, taking in spectacular sunrises over the Atlantic Ocean;

and serene fishing and private boats anchored in the harbor sway gently on the waves.

The village was established 30 miles southeast of Boston by colonists from Plymouth, Massachusetts, in 1636. Despite having direct access to the Atlantic Ocean, the harbor would never become a major hub of business and trade. Navigating into the harbor was difficult, with its shallow depths and long mudflats making it almost impossible for larger ships to dock there. While it wasn't a major seaport, it did become a productive fishing village for local fishermen.

To make navigating into and around the harbor safer, in 1807, local residents petitioned Congress for funding to build a new lighthouse. Congress appropriated $4,000 for the project, which began in 1810. Three men from the nearby town of Hingham—Nathan Gill, Charles Gill, and Joseph Hammond Jr.—were in charge, and the lighthouse was completed and activated in September 1811. The first keeper assigned to man the 25-foot-tall lighthouse was Captain Simeon Bates, who quickly moved into the keeper's house along with his wife, Rachel, and their nine children. Two of those children were daughters Rebecca and Abigail.

One year after the lighthouse first began leading boats in and out of the harbor, President James Madison was at the breaking point with Britain. They had severely limited the United States' ability to trade with European countries, along with the Royal Navy's practice of capturing American seamen in order to fill out crews on British warships. On June 18, 1812, Madison declared war on Britain, and the War of 1812 began.

One year after the United States and Britain had gone to war, a historic battle took place off the coast, near Scituate Harbor. On June 1, 1813, the USS *Chesapeake*, under the command of Captain James Lawrence, engaged the HMS *Shannon* in a fierce fight at sea. During the battle, Lawrence was fatally shot, but his dying words, the last command he would give to his crew, would live on forever as a battle cry of the US Navy: "Don't give up the ship!"

In retaliation for the US declaration of war, the Royal Navy began blockading major US ports up and down the East Coast. Although small fishing villages like Scituate Harbor were not blockaded—as they were not considered strategically important—they still suffered harassment from the British navy. British warships would sail into these small harbors up and down the New England coast, villages with no military protection or land troops, and proceed to raid and ransack them, pilfering livestock, food, and other supplies and then setting any boats in the harbor ablaze, sometimes even the village itself.

The British raiders first came to Scituate Harbor on June 11, 1814. One of their warships anchored offshore and deployed sailors in small boats who then went about setting fire to several fishing vessels at anchor. Onshore, Captain Bates watched the sailors setting the boats alight. He was able to get off two shots from the small cannon located at the lighthouse, in an attempt to scare them away, but it was ineffective. The small boats were out of range, and before long, with their job done, the sailors returned to the British ship and disappeared. The only good thing that came from the encounter was that the village itself was not ransacked.

The British would send ships back to Scituate Harbor two more times over the next few weeks, but each time, the local militia, of which Captain Bates was a member, was able to turn back the British sailors before they wreaked havoc on the village. Still, the British were able to destroy or capture several more boats before leaving the scene. There would be no further attacks by the British for the remainder of the summer. In fact, by autumn, the town's local militia had disbanded so the men could return to their homes to tend to the fall harvest.

Since arriving at the Scituate lighthouse, Captain Bates's daughters, twenty-one-year-old Rebecca and fifteen-year-old Abigail, had whiled away their time by learning how to play the fife and drum. "I was fond of military music and could play four tunes on the fife," Rebecca recalled years later. " 'Yankee Doodle' was my masterpiece."

As September approached, two ships arrived at Scituate carrying an important cargo: flour, which would help the village survive the upcoming harsh New England winter. After their arrival, Captain Bates and his wife, along with most of their children, headed into town for supplies, leaving Rebecca, Abigail, and their younger brother behind to tend to the lighthouse for a few days, something they had done before.

On September 1, 1814, Rebecca glanced out of a window from the keeper's house. To her horror, she spotted a British warship dropping anchor. Immediately, the young woman knew they would need help, to protect not only the village but the two shipments of flour as well. Rebecca dispatched their brother to town to raise the alarm. As she turned back to look out the window again, she spied dozens of British sailors descending over the sides of the ship into boats like armies of ants, marching out of their dirt mounds. She knew by the time help arrived, it would be too late.

Rebecca's first thought was for her and her sister to grab the muskets and ammunition left behind by the former militia and take on the invaders themselves, but at best, they would only be able to pick off one or two of the hordes of sailors approaching from the sea.

Then an idea came to her—an outrageous plan, if ever there was one, a strategy only a good novelist could produce. She told her sister to fetch her drum and she would get her fife. When Abigail questioned what she was up to, Rebecca replied, "We are going to scare them. They will assume that a fife and drum are at the head of a company of soldiers." She warned her sister that to make the plan work, they would have to stay out of sight, because otherwise, the British would "laugh us to scorn."

The two girls took up a position in a thick stand of trees and began playing "Yankee Doodle," Rebecca's favorite tune—quite appropriate for the moment. They watched through the trees as the small boats slowly made their way into the harbor, getting closer and closer to the shore. As they did, the girls played louder, making it sound like a large militia was moving into place.

Suddenly, a single shot was fired from a gun aboard the main British ship and a signal flag was run up the mast. Hearing the music, the captain of the vessel was sending the signal to the sailors to return to the ship, which they promptly did, rowing back to the vessel and climbing back aboard before hauling anchor and sailing away.

This was the last raid to be attempted by the British on Scituate Harbor. The two-girl army had saved the village.

Years after the event, Rebecca and Abigail signed affidavits attesting to the facts of the story. Congress was drafting a bill in 1880 to award the girls a pension of $25 a year for their bravery, but unfortunately, they both died before the bill could be brought to a vote.

The fife that Rebecca played is on display at the lighthouse museum, and visitors to the Scituate Lighthouse say that on a cool autumn night, you can still hear the sounds of a fife and drum being played in the darkness.

FOOTNOTE TO HISTORY: BEFORE UNCLE SAM, THERE WAS BROTHER JONATHAN

The War of 1812 had many long-lasting effects on the United States. First, it ushered in a new feeling of nationalism across the country; instead of considering the states as individual entities, Americans began looking at the country as a single united nation. This feeling was bolstered by the creation of two iconic American symbols: Francis Scott Key's heart-swelling patriotic song that would become the country's national anthem, "The Star-Spangled Banner"; and the man who would emblazon that patriotic message on the hearts of the nation, helping it slog through its battle against Britain, our favorite uncle, Uncle Sam.

But before Uncle Sam was created, there was another cartoon character that personified the courage of the American people. His image was not as stirring as that of Uncle Sam, who was ready for battle, imparting to citizens the need to do what's right for one's country, and to let patriotism ring. This other fellow, named Brother Jonathan, represented the average American, depicted as seemingly a bit slow-witted on the outside, but on the inside, he was cunning, courageous, and determined.

The story of how Brother Jonathan got his name comes from the Revolutionary War. In the 1700s it was quite common to call a friend your "brother." If you had a friend named Joe, you would greet him with a hearty "Good afternoon, Brother Joe." According to one story, "Brother Jonathan" was colloquialized by General George Washington. When he was in need of wise counsel on certain matters, he would turn to the governor of Connecticut, one of the few governors at the time who sided with the patriots' revolution, Jonathan Trumbull. It is said that Washington would often say to his advisors, "Let us consult Brother Jonathan."

One hundred years later, historians would poke holes in that story, but whether or not it's true, there actually was a Brother Jonathan figure. Jonathan was often portrayed in cartoon form in newspapers and almanacs during the Revolution, and also in stage performances. Historians say that the moniker "Jonathan" was used by the British as a derogatory term against the patriots, the "brother" tacked on as the universal greeting for like-minded neighbors.

Unlike other images that attempted to portray the might and determination of the new nation, like Columbia or Liberty, Brother Jonathan was a caricature of a country bumpkin, an average American often portrayed as a peddler or sailor who appeared slow on the uptake but was able to turn the tide on whoever crossed his path with his quick wit and cunning. He was often depicted as coming up against a representation of the pompous and highly educated British gentry in the form of a character named John Bull. In one cartoon, for example, Jonathan is forcing John Bull to drink what was called a "Perry," a drink made from unfermented pear juice that would induce vomiting. The joke was that "Perry" was also the name of Oliver Hazard Perry, the American war hero who defeated the mighty British navy in a battle on Lake Erie. The cartoon made it clear that Brother Jonathan was making John Bull take his punishment from "Perry."

While Brother Jonathan had a quick, sometimes punny, sense of humor, by the War of 1812, he was morphing into a new and more serious-minded political character, and became an image used throughout the war. But as the war progressed, the cartoon simpleton was phased out entirely by a new and more dynamic symbol of America. A meatpacker from Troy, New York, Sam Wilson, was suppling barrels of beef to the US military during the war. Each barrel was stamped with the abbreviation, "U.S." Upon receiving the barrels and seeing the label, soldiers would say they had received a barrel from "Uncle Sam." The name stuck, and became synonymous for anything related to the federal government.

And with that, Brother Jonathan disappeared from history.

· 8 ·

THE FREE STATES OF . . .

March 4, 1861. The newly elected and sworn-in president of the United States, Abraham Lincoln, faced strong opposition from Southern states. Agriculture was the main economic engine that drove the Southern economy. The Southern climate was perfect for growing tobacco and cotton, but growing and harvesting these valued products came off the sweat and backs of enslaved people, who were under the thumb of their captors and saw no possible hope for freedom in their future. With the election of Lincoln, Southern plantation owners saw the writing on the wall, and knew that eventually he would attempt to put an end to slavery.

During his inaugural address on that March day in 1861, Lincoln attempted to ease their fears:

Apprehension seems to exist among the people of the Southern States, that by the accession of a Republican Administration, their property, and their peace, and personal security, are to be endangered. There has never been any reasonable cause for such apprehension. Indeed, the most ample evidence to the contrary has all the while existed, and been open to their inspection. It is found in nearly all the published speeches of him who now addresses you. I do but quote from one of those speeches when I declare that "I have no purpose, directly or indirectly, to interfere with the institution of slavery in the States where it exists. I believe I have no lawful right to do so, and I have no inclination to do so."

Lincoln's attempt to address the issue was ignored for the most part, and beginning with South Carolina ten months later, eleven Southern states seceded from the Union, and the Civil War began.

That is the cut-and-dried version of how the Civil War began, but actually, the feelings among Southerners about the issue of secession were not that simple. Some slave owners took Lincoln at his word, believing that he would not eliminate and free their slaves. Other slave owners wanted to ensure that the institution continued unabated and felt the only answer was to secede from the Union and create their own country. Still others, including John Brown and the daughter of a South Carolina slave owner, Angelina Grimké Weld, fought to put an end to slavery once and for all.

And then there were the average, everyday people who did not own slaves. They owned small farms or businesses and just wanted to be left alone to raise their families in peace but found themselves caught in the middle. There were no reliable polls taken during these times, so we will never know the exact proportion of the Southern population who favored—or feared—secession, but it was clear there were many shades of contrasting views on the subject.

As the war waged on, pockets of resistance to the Confederacy dotted the Southern landscape. Much like the debate on secession, this resistance took shape for several reasons and took on many forms. Some counties in Southern states wanted to remain neutral, taking a "just keep us out of this war" attitude. Others were in full-out rebellion against the Confederacy. Many times the latter group started out leaning more toward being neutral to the fight, but after seeing the devastation that their own Confederate

Army was wreaking across their farms, fields, and families, they took up arms to side with the Union. These renegade counties became generally known as "free states," counties within a state that decided to break away and become independent of the state where they were located—or at the very least, to declare their neutrality during the war.

This is the story of three of those rebellious counties and regions, one of which was so successful with their rebellion that they actually became the country's thirty-fifth state.

In September 1861, the first map of its kind was printed: a visual representation of the 1860 US Census, including the distribution of the slave population in the United States. Created for the US government by Henry S. Graham and Edwin Hergesheimer, the overall map of the country was further broken down by states and their individual counties. The largest section was that of the state of Virginia, the biggest state in the Union at the time.

Virginia was unique in that there was a definitive dividing line between its northwestern and eastern regions, bringing into sharp focus the difference between Northern and Southern states. To the northwest of the Allegheny Mountains, the number of slaves ranged from zero to 4.1 percent of the population. To the east, that number jumped, ranging anywhere from 10 to 65 percent, with the lower percentage being closer to the mountains. That amounted to approximately 18,000 slaves in the west as compared to almost a half million in the east. The reason for this difference was clear: The western counties were more industrial than agricultural, producing iron, coal, salt, and oil. The east had a slave-based agricultural economy, with tobacco being the main crop. Because of this divide, the northwestern counties were more Union-leaning, the east, more toward the Confederacy.

On April 17, 1861, the Virginia statehouse passed the Ordinance of Secession, proposing to leave the Union by a vote of 88 to 55. Of the fifty-five "no" votes, thrity-two came from the counties west of the Alleghenies. Afterward, residents and elected officials in the western counties held a special convention during which they denounced the ordinance's passage. It is during this convention that talk of those counties actually splitting off to become their own independent state within the Union began to circulate.

On May 23, the Ordinance of Secession was put to a vote of the people, and it passed overwhelmingly, 125,950 votes to 20,373. The tally of the "no" votes would have been higher, but many of the ballots cast by the western counties had been discarded. The ordinance had passed and Virginia officially seceded from the Union. Three days later, Union general George McClellan moved his troops into the Union-friendly western counties of the state to preserve the region's valuable natural resources for the North.

A second convention was held in August 1861, in the town of Wheeling, where the Committee on a Division of the State drafted an ordinance calling for the forty-eight western counties to officially break away from Virginia and become their own independent state, the state of Kanawha. On October 24, the ordinance was approved by voters in those western counties, and one month later, a constitution was written for the new state, which was officially renamed West Virginia.

One year after Virginia seceded from the Union, a petition from West Virginia was brought up on the floor of the US Senate to approve the territory as the country's thirty-fifth state. The state's representatives in Washington agreed that the few slaves remaining in West Virginia would gradually be emancipated, and with that, the Senate approved the petition on December 15, 1862. Soon after, President Lincoln officially made West Virginia part of the Union.

Scott County in Tennessee faced the same situation as the western counties of Virginia, but the act that called for the secession of this "free state" from Tennessee didn't resolve with the end of the Civil War. In fact, the independence of this county wasn't dissolved until 1986.

As was the case with the formation of the state of West Virginia, the mountainous landscape of east Tennessee was unsuitable for all but the smallest home farms. According to the Museum of Scott County, the county itself seemed like an afterthought—almost as if Scott County was created from what was left over after the establishment of the adjacent Fentress, Morgan, and Campbell Counties.

Being in a remote, rocky, and mountainous region of the state, where large-scale farming was an impossibility, Scott County had no need for slave labor. The 1860 Census shows that a total of sixty-one slaves were owned in the entire county. So, while secession fever struck the wealthy plantation owners, who pushed for Tennessee to leave the Union, the residents of east Tennessee were against it. The first resolution for the state to split from the Union was voted on by Tennesseans in February 1861, but failed miserably, by a vote of 69,452 to 57,745. Of all the voters in Scott County, 93 percent voted against secession.

Tennessee governor Isham Harris was determined to see his state join the Confederacy, and a second referendum was put to voters three months later. With the Battle at Fort Sumter taking place shortly after the first vote was held, those events in South Carolina and the beginning of the Civil War swung the pendulum, and the second referendum passed handily. Once again, however, the voters of Scott County would have nothing of it, with 97 percent of its voters voting against secession.

The vote to secede so angered voters in the county that they petitioned the governor to allow the state's eastern counties to secede from Tennessee and become their own free and independent state. Harris refused the petition, but it didn't matter. One Scott County resident said, "If the [insert expletive here] State of Tennessee can secede from the Union, then Scott County can secede from the State of Tennessee."

And with that, a special session was held in the county seat of Huntsville and a proclamation was ratified, declaring Scott County independent of Tennessee. The county became the Free and Independent State of Scott. Upon hearing of the petition, state officials pointed out that the county had no legal right to split from the state. County officials replied that if the state had a right to secede from the Union, then Scott County could be independent of Tennessee.

Even though the separation was not legal, the symbolism of the move was a powerful one and would cause this quiet region of Tennessee to experience horrible revenge against its population, perpetrated by outsiders, vigilante raids, and even guerrilla warfare. As a result, the county formed its own militia to take on Confederate troops that were sent to the Scott County with orders to teach the rebel Rebels a lesson. The largest battle between the Confederate Army and county militia took place on August 13, 1862, the Battle of Huntsville.

The governor had dispatched anywhere between 600 and 1,700 troops to the county seat to take out the militia and put an end to the rebellion. The militia was aided with a garrison of Union soldiers, but they were so inexperienced at combat that most of them retreated. With only a handful of Union soldiers and the county militia outnumbered, it didn't take long for the Confederate troops to take control of the county seat. In the process, the soldiers ransacked the town, looting stores and farms. The soldiers tried to locate the county officials who had started the rebellion, but they were never captured. Even though the county militia was defeated, the ordinance proclaiming the county as free and independent of Tennessee was still in effect.

Fast-forward to July 4, 1986: For one reason or another—whether it was because everyone had forgotten that Scott County was still a free and independent state and the declaration of 1861 had never been rescinded, or perhaps because nobody was able to find the documentation that declared the county the Free State of Scott—Scott County was by all accounts still not officially part of Tennessee, or at least, according to the referendum that was passed in 1861.

Scott County was one of the many towns and counties across Tennessee that was celebrating what the state's department of tourism called "Tennessee Homecoming '86," a yearlong celebration that emphasized and promoted the state's history. At the Scott County celebration, amid the music, food, and carnival rides, an unusual event was held. The county commission held a special public meeting and took up only one order of business: a recommendation that the "Free and Independent State of Scott be dissolved and that petition be made to the governor and legislature of Tennessee for readmission into the state of Tennessee as Scott County, Tennessee."

A vote was taken, and with only two dissenting votes, the resolution passed. Soon after, then-governor Lamar Alexander signed the resolution, which read:

> *After 125 years of independence, in this year of the Tennessee Homecoming, the Scott Commissioners and the people of Scott County have declared the Free and Independent State of Scott to be dissolved.*

A better ending to the saga couldn't have been scripted.

Heading back to the year 1860, further south in Jones County, Mississippi, only 12 percent of its population were slaves, making it the smallest percentage in the entire state. For this reason, the residents of Jones County were not particularly keen on fighting in the war, and looked at the Confederacy as being the invading government. Even so, those who disagreed with the war and sided with the Union would still have to take up arms for the Confederacy. A series of conscription laws were enacted by the Confederate government that in essence forced men between the ages of eighteen and thirty-five who were citizens of a state in the Confederacy to either take up arms or face the possibility of being shot as traitors. To make matters worse, with the passing of the Twenty-Negro Law, the war was now seen for what it was: a rich man's war. If a plantation owner owned twenty or more slaves, they were exempt from fighting. As one private, Jasper Collins, wrote, "It [is] a rich man's war and a poor man's fight."

While the men were called off to battle, back home, the situation for many was dire. Shortages of food and clothing were becoming critical, fields were lying fallow, families were starving, and the laws passed by the Confederacy only exacerbated the situation. This included a "tax-in-kind" law, which meant that state tax collectors could show up at a farm or business and take whatever they wanted—horses, chickens, hogs, cloth, flour, anything and everything—which would then be turned over to the army. Confederate colonel William Brown reported what the tax collectors were doing, but his complaints fell on deaf ears. In one report he wrote, "[The tax collectors] have done more to demoralize Jones County than the whole Yankee army."

One Jones County man, Newt Knight, was sent to fight in Vicksburg, but he deserted. He was soon tracked down by authorities, tortured, and his entire farm was destroyed in retaliation. Knight quickly assembled a group of 125 men from Jones and the surrounding counties with the intent of protecting themselves, their families, and farms from the Confederate Army. They were known as the Knight Company.

This militia would hide out in swamps and surprise Confederate troops as they marched into the area. The tactics devised and utilized by the company were extremely effective in disrupting the Confederate Army's movements throughout the region, and prevented further decimation of the men's farms and families. It wasn't long before Confederate president Jefferson Davis received word about the Knight Company. The message relayed to him said that Jones County was in open rebellion and that they had "proclaimed themselves 'Southern Yankees' and [were] resolved to resist by force of arms all efforts to capture them." In Washington, Secretary of War James Seddon received word that the US flag was now flying over the courthouse in Jones County.

The rebellion within the rebellion infuriated Davis, and he dispatched one of his most successful and brutal officers, Colonel Robert Lowry, and his troops to Jones County to root out the traitors. Unleashing packs of bloodhounds, Lowry's men captured many in the Knight Company and returned them to their original Confederate units. Those that were not captured were either mauled by the hounds or were lynched and left hanging in trees as a warning to others. Knight's militia was effectively dismantled.

Newt Knight himself was never captured, eventually returning to his farm. Soon after, his wife left him, but he would remarry, this time to a former slave who had helped the Knight Company in their fight against the Confederacy. Before passing away in 1922, Knight was called upon twice more to provide humanitarian aid and to hand out justice. Following the end of the war, Knight became a commissioner for the US Army, during which time he distributed much-needed food and supplies to the poor and suffering in the South. He also rescued several Black children who were still being held as slaves in nearby Smith County. Knight was later appointed a deputy US marshal for the Southern District.

While Jones County never officially became the "Free State of Jones County," they came as close as they could to making it a reality, thanks to Newt Knight and his Knight Company.

FOOTNOTE TO HISTORY:
THE GREAT STONE FLEET

The first news of a great stone fleet setting sail for Charleston, South Carolina, during the Civil War came from a column that appeared in the *New York Times*, dated November 23, 1861. The article told of a fleet of old whaling ships that had departed New Bedford, Massachusetts, and New London, Connecticut, bound for the Confederate harbor. Before leaving port, the captains of the fleet were given sealed orders that were not to be opened until the harbor pilots had left the vessels and the ships were well out to sea.

The ships were embarking on a secret mission devised by Assistant Secretary of the Navy Gustavus Fox. Charleston, which was referred to by many in the North as a "rat hole," had been a thorn in the side of the Union since Confederates first captured Fort Sumter and set off the chain of events that led to the secession of Southern states from the Union and the beginning of the war. Fox's idea was to sink a group of ships loaded with stones and rocks at the entrance of the harbor to prevent Confederate war and merchant vessels from entering or exiting. The problem was that the harbor did not consist of a single entrance but rather a myriad of channels that snaked their way from the city to the ocean.

No matter. The idea was approved by Secretary of the Navy Gideon Welles, who began secretly purchasing a fleet of old New England whaling vessels. These ships were extremely strong, with double decking, and each weighed ten tons. The navy paid $10 a ton for each ship.

Welles also began purchasing stones and granite—7,500 tons of it, at 50 cents a ton—from local farms, to be used as weight to sink the ships. In the *New York Times* article, the ships were described as having had all of their metal fittings removed and a hole drilled in the bottom in which a 5-inch-wide lead plug was fitted. The idea was to have the ships sail to various locations around the harbor where the lead plugs in each would be removed, causing the ships to sink within twenty minutes, thus blocking entry into the harbor.

At about 3 p.m. on December 19, 1861, the ships arrived in Charleston. A reporter wrote that the "weather was delightful. The sky was belted around the horizon by an exquisite purple haze." The lead plugs were removed, and as the ships began to sink, the crews sawed off the ships' tall masts and then abandoned ship, leaving the hulks to float to the bottom.

This action drew criticism from many critics in the North and around the world, who feared that the ships resting on the bottom would permanently destroy the port, making it unusable after the war had ended. In a *London Times* article dated January 3, 1861, a reporter wrote, "We are told, with a dastardly exultation, that fleets have gone forth from New Bedford and New London . . . [and] have obliterated for years to come the channels of entry by sea of Charleston. . . . The object is not to strangle the great port, but destroy it for all time."

Sixteen ships were either sunk or set on fire that day, effectively blocking the harbor, but as one of the vessels' captains, Charles Henry Davis, had predicted earlier, before the ships had arrived on scene, it was only a temporary solution. The action of the strong currents and fierce storms that the Carolina coast is known for quickly tore apart the wooden ships, with the hulls sinking deep into the sandy bottom. Before long, Charleston Harbor was open again.

· 9 ·

CANADA AND THE
AMERICAN CIVIL WAR

The tide was turning in favor of the Union during the American
Civil War following decisive victories at Gettysburg,
Pennsylvania, and Vicksburg, Mississippi, in 1863. As the third
year of the battle began, it was clear to the president of the
Confederate States, Jefferson Davis, that a plan was needed to
help win back confidence in their cause. An audacious strategy
was hatched in which the Confederacy would attack the North
from, well, the north, but not from within the northernmost states
of the Union, like Maine or Vermont, but rather from the country's neighbor to the north, Canada. While Davis's plan is mostly
relegated to a footnote in the history of the Civil War, when we
take a closer look, we find that Canada actually played an important (if oft-neglected) role in the war.

At the outset of the war, Canada was not a country, per se,
but a federation of British colonies—Canada East (Quebec),
Canada West (Ontario), New Brunswick, Nova Scotia, and Prince
Edward Island. A declaration that recognized these colonies as the
Dominion of Canada would not come for another five years. As
the United States was literally splitting itself in two with brother
fighting brother, the British colonists in Canada were rightfully

concerned about what effect the war would have on their own safety and security. The deep concern and fear Canadians had that the strengthening US military might attempt to take control of the provinces to expand its own territory is one of the reasons the country of Canada was created in the first place, in 1867.

As the American Civil War began, Britain declared itself and the Canadian provinces neutral in the conflict. They had strong economic relationships with the North, and it wasn't only in the form of trade. It is estimated that over 250,000 Canadians were living and working in the United States in 1861. And despite the fact that Britain had abolished slavery in all of its colonies worldwide nearly twenty years earlier, in 1833, and that the British government saw the South as being a belligerent power, they still wanted to maintain trade relations with the Confederacy as well. Cotton was a highly sought-after commodity in England and extremely important to the British economy, so Britain needed to maintain that connection with the South.

In 1861, the city of Montreal was already the financial center of the Canadian provinces. Canada's largest city had established a stable banking system prior to the outbreak of the war but found itself flush with cash during the war years. They had become a clearinghouse for funds from blockade runners who would chance fate by penetrating the gauntlet of US naval ships surrounding Southern port cities in order to bring its valuable commodity, cotton, back to England.

Overall, the majority of Canadians opposed slavery, and the provinces became a safe haven for escaped slaves from the South. The provinces to the north of America had become the final stop on their journey to freedom along what was known as the Underground Railroad, a system of overland and water routes (not an actual railroad) that escaped slaves could take to gain their freedom in either the Northern states or Canada. The former slaves would be aided along their journey by abolitionist

Christians, Native Americans, and free Blacks, or as they called themselves, "conductors," guiding them from one safe location to another, where they were offered food and shelter until they reached their final destination. The conductors referred to the escaped slaves as "cargo" or "freight" heading to the "terminus," or final destination. It is estimated that 100,000 slaves gained their freedom via the Underground Railroad, and between 30,000 and 40,000 of them ended their journey in Canada.

In all, between 33,000 and 55,000 Canadians took up arms and came across the border to fight in the war, mostly on the Union side, and mostly voluntarily. Besides volunteers coming from Canada, the United States saw the provinces as being prime recruiting grounds. In May 1861, shortly after the war began, the United States had established recruiting stations in Montreal and Toronto, offering young Canadian men a shilling and other incentives for signing up.

In addition to official recruiting, there were other unscrupulous recruiters from the United States who used a dubious practice called "crimping"—in essence, taking advantage of unsuspecting victims. The practice is best illustrated by the story of Charles E. Lloyd, an out-of-work Canadian whose family was in dire straits financially.

Lloyd had left his home for the United States in an attempt to find employment in Detroit or Buffalo, but having no luck, he made the decision to return home. Before leaving Buffalo, a man walked up to Lloyd and offered him a drink of liquor. He was suspicious of the offer—after all, he didn't know the man—so he declined. The man offered him a soda instead, which he accepted. The next thing Lloyd knew, he was waking up in a US military camp. He had been drugged and now found himself a member of the US Army. Before his case could be heard as to what had happened to him, Lloyd deserted and presumably headed back to Canada.

Other Canadians wanted to do their part to help the Union by standing up their own militias. Late in 1861, a native of Montreal,

Arthur Rankin, wanted to aid the Union cause by recruiting his own all-Canadian militia. His plan was to recruit 1,600 volunteers that would form a militia he would call the 1st Detroit Regiment of Lancers. The unit would be led by former Canadian officers who had been trained by British officers and had battle experience.

Rankin took his proposal to prominent officials across the border in Detroit. They were so impressed with the plan that they arranged for him to meet with President Lincoln and Secretary of State William Seward. On September 11, 1861, Rankin was given the go-ahead to start forming the Lancers, but the idea was not sitting well with high-profile pro-Confederate officials and newspapers in Canada, who charged Rankin with treason and violating the Foreign Enlistment Act, which forbade British subjects from serving in foreign conflicts. Rankin was arrested in Toronto and put on trial. With no substantial evidence, the charges were dropped and he was released, but those charges, at least in the public's eye, still stood. He was unable to convince enough men to join the Lancers, and recruitment for the regiment dwindled. At the same time, with tensions mounting between Britain and the United States, Canadians were even more wary of joining a militia like the Lancers, and the regiment folded.

The neutrality between the United States, Canada, Britain, and the Confederacy almost ended on November 8, 1861, when a British mail ship, the RMS *Trent*, was captured by an American naval vessel under the command of Captain Charles Wilkes. Without permission from Washington, Wilkes had the *Trent* boarded and searched. What they found surprised them: The former chairman of the US Senate Foreign Relations Committee, James Mason, and New Orleans lawyer John Slidell were on board. The pair had been dispatched by Confederate president Jefferson Davis to work on a deal with Britain and France, whereby the two superpowers would recognize the Confederacy as a sovereign nation, giving their cause legitimacy and opening up more avenues for funding. Wilkes took the envoys prisoner but allowed the *Trent* to continue its voyage to England.

The reaction by Britain was immediate and swift. The government proclaimed the capture of the vessel illegal, declaring that it was in violation of their neutrality. Britain threatened a war with the United States if they did not immediately release Mason and Slidell and issue a formal apology. In the end, cooler heads prevailed. In response to the incident, and Britain's reaction, Lincoln famously said: "One war at a time."

Secretary of State William Seward sent notice to Britain that the United States would release the prisoners, but the only apology was a finessed response: The secretary defended the captain's actions, saying that Wilkes should have captured the entire ship, not just taken the envoys prisoner, and that the courts should decide the legality of the seizure.

While international tensions over the seizing of the shop subsided and war on a second front was averted, Britain recognized that their neutrality in the conflict was tenuous at best and predicted that the United States could begin an invasion of Canada at any moment. Thousands of British troops arrived in Canada shortly after the *Trent* incident to ensure the safety of Canadians.

Not all Canadians sympathized and rooted for the North. There was a large contingent who sided with Southerners, taking umbrage with the US government for forcing their will upon the South. And while Canada was an attractive destination for escaped slaves, it also attracted others, including Canadian Southern sympathizers, Confederate envoys, and escaped Confederate prisoners of war. This loose coalition of men—and women—would gather in hotels and taverns and rail against the Union.

But these meetings were more than just Union-bashing parties. They also served as opportunities to plan raids on the North, to disrupt their economy and their war effort. There were even discussions of plans to kidnap or assassinate President Lincoln.

In the capital of the Confederacy, Richmond, Virginia, President Davis called upon his old friend, Clement C. Clay Jr., a former US senator and now Confederate senator from Alabama, and Mississippi state legislator Jacob Thompson to organize a Confederate secret service. This organization immediately went into action, executing plans to set up volunteers in Canada that would make raids upon the Union from across the border, with the objective of causing enough disruption that the Union would begin considering peace negotiations.

The two men selected by Davis could not have been more opposite. While Clay was tired of war and bloodshed and wanted to work toward peace negotiations, Thompson sought retaliation against the North. Eventually, it was Davis who made the call, writing to Thompson:

> *Considering special trust in your zeal, discretion, and patriotism, I hereby direct you to proceed at once to Canada, there to carry out such instructions as you have received from me verbally, in such manner as shall seem most likely to conduce to the furtherance of the interests of the Confederate States of America.*

To put it simply, as Pulitzer Prize–winning author and historian James McPherson wrote, the letter from Davis gave Thompson the right to "infiltrate across the border into the U.S. and raise as much hell as possible."

Thompson set about recruiting escaped Confederate prisoners and any Southern sympathizers he could muster to form militias that would raid and disrupt the Northern war effort as retaliation for the Union's decimation of the South. Over the next year, he would either organize or fund several schemes to disrupt the Union Army. One of his most audacious plans was to use bioterrorism against the Union.

Shortly after Thompson began organizing his operations, he was contacted by Kentucky doctor Luke Blackburn. Blackburn had received word that there was an outbreak of yellow fever on the island of Bermuda. He was dispatched to the island where he collected clothing from sick patients. He then had the clothes shipped to Halifax, and from there, to merchants in the United States, where the contaminated items would be sold and supposedly infect the population. The problem was that at the time, no one knew that yellow fever was transmitted by mosquitoes and not by contact. Blackburn was eventually arrested and stood trial for violating the Foreign Enlistment Act but was acquitted. He returned to Kentucky where he became the state's governor in 1879.

Thompson's raiders continued to wreak havoc from their bases in Toronto and Montreal. The raiders disrupted the Republican National Convention in Baltimore, during which President Lincoln would be nominated for a second term; they set fire to several theaters in New York City; organized escapes of Confederate soldiers from Union POW camps; and even attacked Union ships sailing Lake Erie.

One of his most famous plans was a simple raid by a band of Confederates into the small Vermont village of St. Albans. Henry Ward Beecher describes St. Albans in his 1868 novel, *Norwood*, as a place where autumn "reaches a climax . . . a place in the midst of greater variety of scenic beauty than any other that I can remember in America." It was against this scenic backdrop that in early October 1864, eighteen (some accounts say twenty-two) men walked into St. Albans and took up lodging where they could find it. The men confidently told anyone who asked that they were visiting from Canada, part of a hunting and fishing group who had come to enjoy the area's outdoor recreation.

By coincidence, the town's sheriff and forty men from the village were in Burlington, Vermont, for a meeting with the state legislature, which meant that St. Albans was not protected by law enforcement. After spending the next few days casing the village, the Confederates set their plan in motion. Just before 2 p.m. on

October 19, 1864, the men ran into the street, each brandishing a pair of .38 caliber pistols. Their leader, Confederate lieutenant Bennett Young, shouted, "In the name of the Confederate States, I take possession of St. Albans!"

Some of the townspeople were rounded up on the village green as the raiders looted the village's three banks of $200,000. Soon, men in the town were running for their guns, and that's when the shooting began. Several people were wounded, both townspeople and raiders. One person was killed, a contractor working on a St. Albans hotel.

The raiders fled the town and the chase was on. The Confederates managed to flee across the border to what they thought would be the safety of Canada, but instead, thirteen of the raiders were captured and put on trial by British authorities. The judge, Charles-Joseph Coursol, heard the evidence and concluded that the raid had occurred on foreign soil, thereby placing it out of his jurisdiction. The captured raiders were released, and the money they had stolen was returned to them.

As you can imagine, anger raged across the United States following their release. The *Chicago Tribune* called for the United States to invade Canada. The *New York Times* wrote that if Britain and Canada "act in a feeble manner and permit the provinces to become . . . a general rendezvous for rebels . . . it will assuredly lead to painful and most undesirable results."

On December 17, Lincoln issued an order calling on Britain and Canada to prevent any further hostile incursions from Canada into the United States and added the requirement that any Canadian entering the country would have to have a passport. Seeing that this action would disrupt the Canadian economy, Britain immediately contacted Lincoln and through negotiations, Lincoln's order was rescinded.

Three months after the raid, it was reported that Thompson had met with "a group of bold men" who had a plan to kill Union leaders, including President Lincoln. Some historians believe that John Wilkes Boothe was one of those meeting with Thompson, but there is no evidence to prove that Thompson ever attended such a meeting. Whether or not he did, didn't matter; Thompson was still charged with conspiring to assassinate the president, but he evaded arrest by fleeing to England, where he stayed in exile until he was exonerated of the charge in 1868, when he returned to the United States, living out the remainder of his life in Memphis, Tennessee.

Relations between the United States, Canada, and Britain in the years immediately following the Civil War were icy at best. Americans were furious with Canada for allowing Jefferson Davis and many of his generals to seek and gain asylum there. They were also angered by the actions of Britain, who allowed Confederate naval vessels to be built in England, which in turn would capture or destroy US Navy ships. The most famous of these was the Confederate cruiser, the CSS *Alabama*, which sank or burned sixty-eight ships in twenty-two months before being sunk off the coast of France in June 1864.

After an investigation, the Senate Foreign Relations Committee sent a bill—known as the *Alabama* Claims (named for the Confederate ship)—for $2.125 billion to Britain, seeking restitution for the damage these ships had caused to US merchant vessels. The two countries met to negotiate terms of an agreement, with the United States suggesting that the provinces of Canada should be swapped in exchange for the cash. In the end, the Treaty of Washington was signed in 1871. This strengthened agreements between the two countries when it came to declaring themselves neutral in a war; prevented neutral powers from allowing hostile nations to use their ports for shipbuilding or outfitting; and required Britain to pay the United States $15.5 million in gold for the damages caused by the CSS *Alabama*.

FOOTNOTE TO HISTORY: SOLDIER GIRL

The next time you see a photo of a tough-looking Civil War soldier dressed in uniform posing for the camera with gun or sword in hand, take a closer look. That soldier boy might just be a soldier girl.

The general historical overview of the Civil War paints a picture of it being a man's war. Men took up their guns and were either drafted, volunteered, or forced into service to fight the incredibly bloody battles while the women were relegated to maintaining the farms back home or acting as nurses for the wounded. The truth is that women, on both the Union and Confederate sides, took up arms themselves to fight.

Despite it being illegal on both sides for women to join their respective militaries, some felt the need to fight for their side's cause. The women would trim their hair, do whatever was necessary to hide their sex, and use false, masculine names to gain entry into the war. Some of the women included Mary Owen—or, as she was known on the battlefield, John Evans. Mary (or John) served for eighteen months in the Union Army before being wounded in the arm and having her cover blown. Confederate officer Lieutenant Harry Buford was in reality Loreta Velazquez. John Williams with the Union's 7th Missouri Infantry turned out to be nineteen-year-old Mrs. S. M. Blaylock, who, when her identity was uncovered, was immediately discharged.

A wonderful story of one of these "soldier girls" is that of Private Franklin Thompson who fought with the Union's 2nd Infantry Unit. Thompson was, in reality, Canadian-born Sarah Evelyn Edmonds.

Edmonds's brother was epileptic and, as such, could not help on the family farm. Sarah's father made her do much of the work that her brother could not do. She enjoyed the physical labor and was described as energetic and adventurous. She loved to ride horses, became an excellent marksman, and was a strong swimmer. When her family arranged for her to marry an older man at the age of fifteen, she ran away and soon disappeared, taking up the male identity of "Frank Thompson."

After moving to Flint, Michigan, where she worked as a successful Bible salesperson, the Civil War broke out, and Sarah made the decision to volunteer to fight with the Union Army. So how did Sarah pass the physical required to join the military? The requirements were hardly stringent: Volunteers must not be blind or lame; they must have all of their limbs and not be subject to having fits. They were not required to strip down, only to have a firm handshake. Sarah, with her abilities, was a shoe-in to pass the physical.

Sarah was able to remain incognito by bathing in streams and creeks near the troop's encampments and sleeping in her clothes. While she was assigned to being the regiment's "male" nurse, she did encounter the realities of war, taking part in both battles of Bull Run, as well as those in Fredericksburg and Antietam. After these battles, she volunteered to become a Union spy. Shaving her head, donning a curly wig, and painting her exposed skin with silver nitrate, she posed as a slave named "Cuff" and infiltrated a group of

Black laborers working in a Confederate camp in Yorktown. After overhearing Confederate plans for an attack, she slipped away in the cover of darkness and relayed the intelligence to the Union Army, who made a surprise attack on the Rebels and scored an impressive victory.

Eventually, Sarah deserted because she had contracted malaria and did not want to have her cover blown. She relinquished her identity of Frank Thompson and married. When she attended the regiment's reunion, the men were shocked and surprised that Frank Thompson was actually Sarah Edmonds.

In all, it is estimated that more than four hundred women fought during the Civil War, but that number is only an approximation. No one really knows for sure how many of the men on enrollment records were actually women.

· 10 ·

THE GREAT CIVIL WAR BREAD RIOTS

On January 9, 1790, just over eight months into his term as the first president of the United States, George Washington said of the newly established country that this republic was "the last great experiment for promoting human happiness." Almost one hundred years later, that experiment was put to the test, stressed almost to the breaking point as the great Civil War broke out, dividing the loyalties of families and tearing the nation into two opposing factions.

The war would last four seemingly endless years, during which time a total of 620,000 people were killed, a number equal to the total number killed during the Revolutionary War, the War of 1812, the Mexican War, the Spanish-American War, World War I, and World War II combined.

Death and suffering was not confined only to the battle-field. The home front, most notably in the Confederacy, suffered greatly. Southern women in particular were finding it difficult to keep their children fed and clothed while their husbands were off fighting the war, to the point where they felt they had no other choice but to take matters into their own hands.

From the fall of Fort Sumter in April 1861 to the subsequent secession of the state of South Carolina soon after, a domino effect was set in motion. One by one, eleven states would break away from the Union, threatening the end of the "Great Experiment." At the outset of the war, the South had predicted the North would experience great suffering from a shortage of food and other supplies, a view that was echoed by many of the politicians and military officers of the Confederacy regarding what effect the war would have on the Northern economy. However, while the Union did experience some deprivation during the war, the prophecy was misplaced, and overall, the economy in the North boomed. Instead, it was the Confederacy that suffered the most.

There were many things that led to the events of the spring and summer of 1863. The first was that the inflation rate in the South had skyrocketed. When the Civil War broke out in 1861, the Confederacy set about printing their own currency. At the time, one Confederate note was worth one gold dollar. By February of 1863, it took $3 in Confederate notes to buy $1 of gold, an inflation increase of 200 percent, making the purchase of goods and food nearly impossible for the poor.

During this time, many of the South's farms were devastated by a prolonged drought; a severe winter with deep and isolating snowfalls (Richmond, Virginia, reported twenty measurable snowfalls in 1862 and 1863, with some dropping over a foot of snow); floods; and the war itself. Farmers were afraid to bring their produce and livestock to the market for fear of impressment by both Union and Confederate armies. If their crops were not taken by the armies, then they would be destroyed during battles or wiped clean by troops foraging their fields. And then there was the Union blockade of Southern seaports that began immediately as each Southern state left the Union, blocking the shipment of goods both in and out of the South.

When Southerners were fortunate enough to get meat, it was in extremely limited supply. People would have to get up before dawn and rush to the market to stake their place, hoping the supply didn't run out before they made it to the front of the line. If they could get meat, they weren't able to preserve it: The salt used in the process was almost nonexistent, since it was produced and shipped down from the North, and what made its way into the Confederate states was too expensive for the average person to buy.

Now, don't think that the entire Confederacy was starving; for the most part, those with means fared well. One resident, Mrs. Cornelia McDonald, wrote that she was living on bread and water while her neighbor "dined sumptuously."

As the war dragged on into its second year, the women of the South demanded action to save their families from starvation. Women organized groups that rioted and raided stores in Arkansas, Georgia, and North Carolina. The riots were referred to by several names: the "Thursday Riot" (so called for the day of the week on which it occurred); the "Holy Women's Riot"; and, more commonly, the "Bread Riots."

The largest of the bread riots occurred on April 2, 1863, in the Confederacy's capital city, Richmond, Virginia. Richmond was unique because, up to this point, its population had swelled not only with thousands of government workers, military officers, and troops moving in but also tourists and onlookers who wanted a glimpse of the war. This increased population made feeding the residents of the city even more difficult.

The April riot began the preceding month when the wife of a Confederate soldier and peddler at the local market, Mary Jackson, began recruiting women for a protest. By April 1, the group had increased to three hundred in number. On that day, with the aid of Minerva Meredith and a group of women who worked in Confederate ordinance factories in the area, the women met at the Belvidere Hill Baptist Church. The gathering ended with the women resolving to demand a meeting with the state's governor, John L. Letcher, the following day, to discuss their plight.

The next morning, the women gathered at the city's George Washington statue and marched to the governor's mansion. From here, the story gets murky. Some accounts say that the governor refused to meet with the women and they returned to the statue. Other accounts say that the governor did meet with the women, but they were not satisfied with his response. In any event, the women did eventually reconvene at the statue where they began marching to the city's business district on Ninth Street.

As the procession made its way through the city streets, its numbers grew. Some accounts put the number at one thousand women and children, while others say it was closer to three thousand. Out of those, it's not clear how many were protesters and how many were onlookers. A visitor to the city, John B. Jones, wrote in his diary:

Not knowing the meaning of such a procession, I asked a pale boy where they were going. A young woman, seemingly emaciated, but yet with a smile, answered that they were going to find something to eat. I could not, for the life of me, refrain from expressing the hope that they might be successful; and I remarked they were going in the right direction to find plenty in the hands of the extortioners.

Eyewitness accounts say that the anger in the women grew with each step they took. Chants of "Bread or blood!" and "We are starving!" rang out just before the mob began breaking down the doors and windows of the shops that lined the street. Jones continued in his diary:

The throng then moved through the city, going store to store, where "they proceeded to empty them of their contents" and didn't leave until they had carts full of flour, meal, clothing, and the staples needed to survive.

As the women continued looting whatever they could get their hands on—primarily food and clothing, but also nonessentials like jewelry—Richmond mayor Joseph Mayo arrived on the scene. He tried to calm the situation, but when he was ignored, he literally read the women the riot act and threatened that the military stationed around the city would come in and start shooting. The riot continued, and soon, the governor and Confederate president Jefferson Davis arrived. In her account of the situation, Davis's wife, Varina Davis, wrote that her husband pleaded with the women to stop and again threatened military intervention. Some eyewitnesses said that Davis actually threw money from his own pockets at the women.

After ransacking the business district, the women finally dispersed, but officials feared another uprising, so cannons were stationed along the city's main thoroughfares. The riot was officially over two hours after it began. Confederate Secretary of War James A. Seddon begged the local newspapers not to print the story of the riot for fear it would be used by the Union as propaganda. It didn't matter. Confederate deserters and Union prisoners of war who were being held in the city and were released soon after the riot told the tale, and it appeared on the front page of the *New York Times* on April 8, 1863.

One of the last bread riots to occur in the Confederacy was in the Gulf Coast city of Mobile, Alabama. Mobile was one of the few major Southern cities to be spared the devastations of war, but its residents still felt the pain and suffering brought on by shortages, mostly due to its port being blockaded.

Prior to the war, during what is known as the Antebellum period (a Latin word that literally means "before the war"), Mobile was a booming seaport where goods were shipped from the North down the numerous rivers that led to the city. The goods would then ship out to other cities around the Gulf Coast and countries in the Caribbean, South and Central America, and Mexico.

The city's main source of income, however, came from serving as a major shipping conduit for the South's prime commodity, cotton. Bales of cotton would be shipped down the Mobile and Tensaw Rivers from the Black Belt area of Montgomery and Selma to the port city, where it would ship out to neighboring states and countries.

Plantation owners became incredibly wealthy from "King Cotton," and the town exuded the quintessential image of a Southern city, with rows of majestic oaks draped in flowing, green Spanish moss, and fragrant, flowering white magnolia trees lining paths around Victorian-era mansions with grand spiral staircases. At the same time, the workers that moved the cotton led mediocre lives at best, happy to have steady work, but living on the edge financially. White laborers, free Blacks, and slave labor had little hope of prospering from the boom, and all felt the pinch. The Union blockade of the city saw shipping come to a grinding halt, crippling the city's economy.

The squeeze that the blockade put on the city was felt at the outset of the war. Food and clothing shortages became more prevalent. Even the simplest of items, such as coffee, were in short supply, and residents began making substitutes with whatever they had available. For example, one such stand-in for coffee was introduced by a resident who wrote in to the local newspaper, the *Mobile Advertiser and Register*:

> *For a family of seven or eight persons, take a pint of well toasted corn meal, and add to it as much water as an ordinary sized coffee-pot will hold, and then boil it well. We have tried this toasted meal coffee, and prefer it to Java or Rio, inasmuch as genuine coffee does not suit our digestive organs, and we have not used it for years. Many persons cannot drink coffee with impunity, and we advise all such to try our recipe. They will find it more nutritious than coffee and quite as palatable.*

In addition to the Union blockade, the situation was exacerbated for Mobilians by the Confederate Army, who prohibited the export of corn out of adjacent states to help the city. Colonel John Pemberton specifically told Mobile that he halted the shipment of corn to the city in order to conserve the supply for his troops and Mississippi's own population. Between the blockade, stonewalling by the Confederacy itself, and profiteering and hoarding by individuals in the city, inflation skyrocketed to 750 percent going into 1863. It was reported in the local newspaper that a pound of butter cost $3.50 and a barrel of flour, $400. Even oil to light the city's streetlights was too expensive, and the city resorted to refilling them with pitch and hard pine knots.

In August of 1863, residents of Mobile were feeling the pain of starvation and want, and much like in Richmond, the fuse was lit for rebellion. One soldier's wife wrote a letter to the local newspaper, the *Mobile Register*, airing her frustration about those profiteering from the plight of the city's citizens:

> *We would make it convenient to close the doors of these extortioners in goods as well as everything else; the blockade goods do a poor man's family no good whatever. They have not enough money to buy a yard, to say nothing of a bolt of calico, domestic, or any other kind of goods. Our good Christian dealer in cloth cannot take the trouble to cut a bolt, he is losing too much money and time. I will be glad, Mr. Editor, for you to tell me who can wear these men's goods, save the families of their brother speculators. This thing has to stop.*

In early September, Mobile mayor R. H. Slough wrote a letter that appeared in the same paper, asking that the wealthiest in the city do their part:

> *In order to relieve the distress, which is known to exist in Mobile, the undersigned would again make an appeal to the citizens. Much has*

been accomplished by means of the Free Market, but much remains to be done, and I think I may with confidence expect that the charitable and Christian spirit of our people will be untiring in its efforts to furnish relief where it may be needed among the worthy and industrious. It is not necessary to give instances. They are known to the actively benevolent of the public. All that I can do is to point the way by which the end may be attained.

I would suggest, therefore, that subscriptions be taken up, and that the work be prosecuted with vigor until such time as at least enough shall be done to supply the wants of those who have claims on the community and worth on the public. There are many indigent women especially who need succor. Their own wants and those of their children are calculated to touch the hardest and least sympathetic heart. Let us then, my fellow citizens, see that these worthy objects of charity are placed above the reach of absolute destitution. Money for the purpose left at my office, or at that of Capt. D. Wheeler, will be devoted to the purpose with care, so that it may reach the necessities of the most deserving.

On September 4, 1863, the women of Mobile had had enough. They organized on the city's Springhill Road with every intention of marching downtown and taking what they needed to survive. A reporter with *The Era* (New Orleans) described the throng as a "most formidable riot by a long-suffering and desperate population."

The women held signs in protest, and once again the chant of "Bread or blood!" and "Bread and peace!" rang out in the streets. Some of the women brandished hatchets, bricks, and axes which they used to enter shops in the town's business district, Dauphin Street.

Seeing what was about to transpire, Slough requested Confederate general Dabney H. Maury to bring in the army and put down the riot by any means necessary. The army did move in, but when given the order to attack the women, the soldiers replied, "If we took any action, [we would] rather assist those starving wives, mothers, sisters and daughters of men who had been forced to fight the battles of the rebellion."

Another military group, the Mobile Cadets, were then ordered to move in and use force to disperse the women. According to *The Era*, the cadets were only a fancy parading unit. The reporter described the cadets' encounter with the women as being "quite a little scrimmage [which resulted] in the repulse of the gallant fellows."

The women had won the battle with the cadets and continued to march on the town. Left with no other choice, Mayor Slough tried to negotiate with the women, promising them that if they would disperse and head back to their homes, their needs and demands would be met. The women believed the mayor and started for home, but later in the evening, tensions rose again as the women believed they were being had. Once again, they headed back to Dauphin Street with renewed anger, this time emptying the stores of clothing, food, and household goods.

And where were the police during all of this? Aiding the women. According to the report in *The Era*, the police and many of the male residents that were not fighting the war came to the women's aid:

> *In coming down Dauphine* [sic] *Street, two women went into a Jew* [sic] *clothing store, in the performance of the work connected with their mission. The proprietor of the store forcibly ejected the intruders, and threw them violently down on the sidewalk. A policeman who happened to be near thereupon set upon the Jew and gave him a severe beating.*

The women of Mobile vowed that if their needs were not met or the war did not end soon, they would burn the city down. Much like the Richmond riot, in a few hours it was over and calm returned to the city. The mayor established a committee to tend to those in need, scouring the city for pockets of poor and destitute citizens so they could distribute funds donated by the wealthy, to be used to buy provisions.

Despite the city's best efforts, the shortages continued to the end of the war and beyond, during Reconstruction. City officials made every effort to aid those in need, and there were no further uprisings by the women of the South.

FOOTNOTE TO HISTORY: THE DRAFT RIOTS OF 1863

To casual readers of American history, when it comes to the American Civil War, it may seem that the war was clear-cut: The South wanted to maintain slavery; Fort Sumter was attacked; Southern states seceded from the Union; men in the North took up arms to preserve the country, while in the South, they took up arms to form new Confederate States.

But as we have seen, the war was much more complicated than that, with many twists, turns, and nuances. For instance, there were those in the North who held their own rebellion of sorts when the US government began drafting men for the army, a move that caused large protests involving violence and death.

On January 1, 1863, President Abraham Lincoln solidified the Union position on the war. With the Emancipation Proclamation, the war officially became about more than just preserving the Union— it was also about the abolishment of slavery. And to win the war, the Union needed more soldiers. In response, Congress enacted the Conscription Act of 1863, the first military draft in the nation's history, in which male citizens (and immigrants who had applied for citizenship) between the ages of twenty-five and forty-five would be required to join the ranks.

But the act was very lopsided. It held that if a man could pay $300, he could either avoid the draft or buy a substitute to take his place.

When the first draft was held in July 1863, many in the North saw it as a violation of their civil liberties and personal freedom. A diverse coalition of ideologies merged together to protest the draft, including people who were racists and anti-Black, those who railed against the rich and powerful, and now, those who had a deep hatred for Lincoln's Republican Party. Groups of Democrats across the Union pledged to "resist to the death all attempts to draft citizens into the army," while New York governor Horatio Seymour predicted that the draft would result in mass mob violence.

He was right. Several large and violent protests erupted across the Union states, but none as deadly as the New York City riot. On July 11, 1863, the first draft in the city was held. Two days later, a mob of one hundred men formed at the recruiting station and violence broke out, with countless injured and the building ransacked and set on fire. Firefighters who attempted to fight the blaze were attacked by the mob, as were policemen and soldiers. African Americans were beaten, tortured, and even lynched and set afire on the streets.

The massacre continued for three days and was not squelched until the US Army, including a garrison that had recently fought in the Battle of Gettysburg, and the state militia moved in to tamp down the violence and restore order. In the end, fifty buildings were destroyed, two thousand people were injured, and over one hundred were killed in the New York City draft riot of 1863.

▪ 11 ▪

THERE'S A
MOLE AMONG US

Preserving history, especially when it comes to paper artifacts, can be a delicate proposition. Documents can yellow, decay, and turn to dust with the slightest change in temperature, humidity, or light. Oil from a person's hands can permanently damage its sensitive surface. And then there is nature itself, animals and bugs that can chew through and destroy history in no time at all. And those are only some of the challenges that the conservators at the National Archives in Washington, DC, face on a daily basis.

Of late, the National Archives has received more attention than ever before with a controversy stemming from the returning of classified documents by a former president. For the most part, however, the National Archives is a quiet sanctuary that most people never think of, even though its importance in preserving American history is paramount. The Archives is an independent federal agency that preserves not only official government documents such as the Declaration of Independence, presidential records, and transcripts of congressional hearings but also personal accounts of historic events, even stories of the everyday lives of average Americans. In turn, those records, and the amassed knowledge within, are shared with the public.

The National Archives building, whose designer, architect John Russell Pope, described as being a "temple to history," is impressive to say the least, as you would expect, coming from the man who also designed the Jefferson Memorial. According to officials with the National Archives, Pope designed the building to give all those who visit a feeling of awe and reverence for the history housed within. A majestic domed rotunda, typical of the Washington governmental landscape, towers above as you walk through the 40-foot-tall bronze doorway. You get the feeling that our history is safe and secure here. The building first opened its doors in 1936 when it received its first rather mundane transfer of records from the US Food Administration, Sugar Equalization Board, and US Grain Corporation.

Since that time, the National Archives has amassed quite a collection, and on a daily basis, conservators work diligently to protect it. Human interaction with the documents, photographs, artwork, and so forth is fairly easy to handle, but then you have to combat furniture beetles that bore holes into all types of wood, case-bearing clothes moths that love to eat and destroy carpets and all manner of fabrics, and, of course, the threat of dampness that can cause mold. But what do you do when you come across a mole in some archival documents?

A mole? How can that be, you ask?

Well, it's not as it seems. The National Archives did not have a mole infestation problem. Rather, this is a fascinating tale about pensions that were promised to Civil War veterans, and more specifically, their widows, and the difficulties many of these women faced when it came to receiving those benefits.

Today, most Americans believe that we should thank veterans who have signed up to defend our democracy by providing benefits once their enlistment is over. It could be as simple as guaranteeing a home loan, providing educational benefits or health care for those wounded in action, or death benefits for survivors of those who died in the line of duty. When the Civil War was entering its second year in 1862, a controversial law was passed by Congress, the Pension Act of 1862. The law, at the time considered the "most liberal pension law ever enacted by [the] government," was the first assistance program enacted to help veterans of war, their widows, and their children. While it was hailed by many, others saw it as an "extravagant, if not unsupportable annual burden."

The act provided private soldiers who were totally disabled with $8 a month, which was later increased to $20 a month. "Total disability" was defined as the loss of a limb or its extremity. All other injuries were up for debate as to how they should be classified. The stipulation was that a veteran would receive a pension only beginning from the time they applied, not from the time they became disabled, so it could be years between their injury and the time they filed the paperwork. That rule changed in 1879, when the law was updated to provide veterans with a lump sum payment that would cover the time they were discharged from service due to an injury to the date they applied, when their regular benefits would kick in. The federal pension system provided not only for White veterans but for Blacks as well, and for the widows of veterans, but the process for filing and receiving the benefits was daunting.

Wounded Black veterans were more often than not denied their pension because to complete the application, they needed to have documentation from a hospital of their injury and the cause of the injury. Blacks were less likely to be hospitalized for their wounds during the war. And to further complicate matters, many did not have enough money to complete the application process, and if they did, White intermediaries reviewing their claims would often reject them without fear of repercussion.

There were also rules for widows. First, she had to be married to the vet at the time of his death, and his death must have been in the line of duty. After her husband died, she was also not permitted to remarry, or her claim would be denied. Commissioner of pensions James Heaton Baker said of the rule requiring that women could not remarry: "Widows, in increasing numbers, cohabit without marriage . . . for fear of losing their pensions," and that others "openly live[d] in prostitution for the same object." He also said that this rule put the government in the "strange attitude of offering a premium upon immorality, of which it should be relieved."

Some of these rules were relaxed in 1890 with yet another revision to the Pension Act of 1862, which allowed widows to receive their husbands' benefits if the vet was disabled for any reason, even if it was not war-related, at the time of his death. In 1901, the law was changed to allow widows to remarry and still receive benefits.

So what does this have to do with the National Archives and a mole? The story is told by an Archives staff member who was assisting a researcher looking into Civil War widows' pensions. The documents they were scouring through were found in the Archives' Civil War Widows Certificate Approved Pension Case File. They were puzzled when they pulled the file. It was rather thick and bulky, but not like it was overstuffed with papers. Gently opening the folder and sifting through the papers, they discovered what was hidden between the documents inside, what the National Archives describes as one of the most unusual items they have ever found: the preserved skin of a mole.

The staff member began researching this odd find and discovered that it was, indeed, intended to serve as documentation to prove that a widow's claim to her husband's pension was legitimate. Research revealed that the insectivore originally belonged to James J. Van Liew, a Union soldier. From what they discovered, Liew's regiment had pitched camp in an area that unfortunately for the soldiers had uninvited guests: moles. Van Liew decided to put an end to one of the "guests" lodging in his tent. He captured it, killed it, and skinned it. For some unknown reason, he decided to write a letter to his wife Charity and send the mole's skin to her. A souvenir of the war? Surely not a token of his affection, but as it turned out, it would prove valuable to his wife, who kept the wartime memento for years after her husband had died.

Following her husband's death, Charity Van Liew filed for her husband's pension. The first thing asked of her, like all widows, was proof that she was in fact married to James J. Van Liew at the time of his death. Simple enough, right? Keep in mind that the couple was married during a time when archiving marriage records was extremely inconsistent, meaning that many records were lost or filed incorrectly. The answer for Charity was to send the letter her husband had written to her that accompanied the mole skin. The problem was, she had kept the skin but had lost the accompanying letter. So, she did the next best thing and sent the mole skin to the Pension Bureau.

With the aid of four friends who wrote letters to the Pension Bureau, testifying that they had seen her husband's letter that accompanied the mole skin, and that the letter had begun with the words, "Dear wife," the Bureau granted her request to begin receiving the pension. Now whether or not the mole skin had anything to do with granting the request is anybody's guess, but you have to assume that it must have had a little something to do with it; after all, how many requests did they receive as unusual as this one?

Today, the mole skin resides in the National Archives, peacefully preserved, pressed between protective sheets in Charity Van Liew's pension application file. The Civil War Widows Certificate Approved Pension Case File is still extremely thick, even without the skin. When the Civil War pension law went into effect, a total of 7,916 people applied, with 2,766 of those being widows. By 1885, the total number of pensioners was 324,968, with 80,767 of those being widows.

The last person to receive a government pension for a family member's service during the Civil War died on May 31, 2020, at the age of ninety. Her name was Irene Triplett.

Irene Triplett's father, Moses "Mose" Triplett, fought for the Confederacy, but in 1863, after becoming ill on a march through Virginia, heading toward Gettysburg, Triplett was hospitalized and missed the battle, which was fortunate. Of the 800 men in his regiment, 734 were either captured, wounded, or died in the battle. Triplett decided to switch sides, taking up arms with the Union, as grandson Charlie Triplett said, so he could "get a pension."

Triplett was discharged in 1865 and returned home to North Carolina. In 1923, his first wife passed away, and in 1924, at the age of eighty-three, he married Elida Hall, who was thirty-three at the time. The couple lost three babies before his daughter Irene was born six years after they were married. In a 2011 article that appeared in the Wilkes County (South Carolina) Genealogical Society newsletter, Irene Triplett said that growing up, her life was difficult. She had no memories of fun, of receiving presents, of having friends or speaking with neighbors. Her family was very isolated. Children at school taunted her, often shouting at her that her father was a traitor. When her father died, his tombstone simply read, "He was a Civil War soldier."

Irene, who suffered from a cognitive disability, and her mother lived in a poorhouse until they were finally able to move to a nursing home. Her mother died in 1997, and because of her disability, Irene was able to receive her father's pension—$73.13 a month—becoming the last recipient of a Civil War pension.

FOOTNOTE TO HISTORY:
A HAIRY SITUATION

While finding a mole skin tucked away neatly in a folder at the National Archives is an unusual find, the Smithsonian Museum of American History thrives on such unique discoveries. They not only preserve important American artifacts but also celebrate anything that paints a picture of life in the United States over the centuries. One such artifact was created by a fellow named John Varden, a presidential hair collector.

Before there was a Smithsonian Museum, there was the National Institution for the Promotion of Science. Located inside the Old Patent Office Building in Washington, DC, the National Institution collected "curious and strange articles presented by individuals . . . articles of immense value." Inside the building, you could find war clubs from Fiji; a Pacific Islander's matted wig used as a helmet during battle; a set of teeth taken from prisoners by one of Fiji's chiefs, made into a necklace; and neck ornaments made of human hair from the island of Tonga. And that was only for starters.

Varden was a former theater actor turned archivist who was working at the National Institution in 1850 when he began his quest to collect locks of hair from the first fourteen US presidents. It's unknown exactly how he acquired the samples. The most plausible answer would be that he contacted friends and relatives of the former presidents, requesting a sample for his collection. Keeping a lock of a loved one's hair after they had passed away has been a long-held tradition, one still practiced today. It is a simple way for grieving families to hang on to the memory of their loved one.

Varden collected hair from fourteen presidents: Washington, John Adams, Van Buren, Jefferson, Harrison, Madison, Tyler, Monroe, Polk, John Q. Adams, Taylor, Jackson, Fillmore, and Pierce. Once completed, it didn't take Varden long to realize that he had a display of enormous historical value, one the public would love to see.

With great care, Varden took each lock, tied them as neatly as he could into a bow, and mounted them on a black background. He then took those locks and arranged them in an 18-by-13-inch ornate frame. He fashioned a label, which was displayed beneath each lock, including the president's name, birth and death dates, and the years they had served in office. He began showing the display to the public in and around the Washington, DC, area, and eventually donated his "Hair of the Presidents, Washington, DC, Collection" to the National Institution, in 1855.

In 1883, the collection was officially transferred to the newly formed Smithsonian Institute, where it remains on display to this day.

· 12 ·

SLAVES CAN BE FREE . . .
JUST NOT HERE

The issue of slavery was at the core of the American Civil War, but it had vexed the country ever since the first Europeans landed on its shores, long before it became a country. Always bookending the discussion of slavery were the pro-slavery voices on one side, in favor of continuing the practice, and on the other, the abolitionists who wanted to see slavery completely eradicated from the country.

But the discussion was not always so unequivocal. There were plenty of gray areas where these philosophies often overlapped, creating a patchwork of ideas about how to deal with the issue, along with the country's original sin, racism. There were many opinions, dating back to the country's origin, when the Framers of the Constitution tried to balance the main tenet of the Declaration of Independence, that "all men are created equal." It was an enormous contradiction, proclaiming that all men are equal, while at the same time allowing human beings to be enslaved and treated brutally by their captors. But if slavery were abolished, many White people believed there was no feasible way they could live side by side with freed African Americans.

An idea that sprouted from these discussions, one that a sitting president and a future president agreed would be the ultimate solution to the problem, was colonization: a means of giving Blacks, both enslaved and free, complete freedom—just not here in the United States. Rather, they would be given their own country, either returned to their original homeland, or placed on some Caribbean island. For White Americans, colonization would provide easy relief when it came to the challenges of emancipating slaves and integrating them into American life, as equals.

While the idea of colonization initially appealed to free Blacks, as well, their opinion of the proposal soon changed. They decided they would rather make a go of it in the land that was now their home, and that promised "all men are created equal."

The idea of colonization had been floated around since the late eighteenth century and was actually conceived by free Blacks, who believed there was no plausible way they would ever enjoy total freedom and justice in America. One of colonization's main proponents at the time was businessman and ship captain Paul Cuffe. After hearing about the slave rebellion on the island of Haiti, the Haitian Revolution, and the liberation of the island's enslaved people, Cuffe was certain that freed slaves and free Blacks in America could do the same. They could emigrate across the ocean to "establish a prosperous colony in Africa," one that would afford them complete freedom and justice, and where their work would power the colony's economy.

In 1807, tensions between the United States and Britain were rising once again, and the United States placed an embargo on imported British goods. Five years later, only months before the War of 1812 began, Cuffe set his ship on a course for the British colony in Africa, the Providence of Freedom, later called Sierra Leone, to research the plan's viability. Sierra Leone was established by Britain as a country made up of free slaves, much as Cuffe had envisioned for slaves in America.

Upon his return to the United States on April 12, 1812, Cuffe's ship and cargo were seized by US Customs for allegedly violating the 1807 embargo. When Customs refused to return the ship, Cuffe took his case to the higher-ups—and you couldn't get much higher than the president of the United States, James Madison. Cuffe met with Madison in the White House, the first time an African American had met with a sitting president, where he made his case as to why his vessel and cargo should be returned to him. He also spoke of the concept of colonization.

Madison agreed that Cuffe's ship should be returned. He also saw something in Cuffe's concept of a nation made up entirely of freed slaves and began corresponding with the captain about how the plan could be put into effect.

With the support of the free Black community throughout the United States and the ear of the US president, on December 10, 1815, Cuffe and his ship, the *Traveler*, set sail for Sierra Leone with thirty-eight African Americans on board, ranging in age from six months to sixty years old, with the intention of relocating them to Africa. It was the first time African Americans had emigrated back to Africa from the United States.

One year later, several prominent Americans—including Daniel Webster and Francis Scott Key, and with the backing of now former president James Madison and current president James Monroe—formed the American Colonization Society (ACS), to expand the concept of colonization. The ACS was made up of an eclectic group of members often at odds with one another; some were pro-slavery, while others were abolitionists. While their goals may have been different, they all agreed that colonization was not only about slaves. Their belief was that free Blacks would never have equal rights in America; colonization would offer them their only chance at obtaining justice, at the same time giving them the chance to escape racism. Not coincidentally, it would also give White Americans a means of dodging the issue of integration. For pro-slavery advocates, it would eliminate the possibility that free Blacks would cause an uprising among the remaining slaves.

Their dream of having African Americans emigrate back to Africa was short-lived. Just two years later, it was evident that free Blacks across the country were beginning to lose interest in the plan. Still, the idea was not yet totally dead. The future sixteenth president of the United States, Abraham Lincoln, had something to say about colonization.

Lincoln believed that allowing slavery to continue in America made a mockery of the nation's guiding principle—that all men are created equal—but at the same time, he admitted he was uncertain how to end slavery. On October 16, 1854, six years before his election as president, Lincoln addressed the issue in a speech delivered in Peoria, Illinois:

> *When it is said that the institution [slavery] exists and that it is very difficult to get rid of it, in any satisfactory way, I can understand and appreciate the saying. I surely will not blame them [Southern people] for not doing what I should not know how to do myself. If all earthly power were given me, I should not know what to do, as to the existing institution. My first impulse would be to free all the slaves, and send them to Liberia—to their own native land.*

Shortly after the start of the Civil War, in 1861, Fort Monroe in Virginia became a "safe haven" for escaped slaves. The fort's commander, General Benjamin F. Butler, declared that escapees were contraband of war and would not be returned to their owners. While the fort was considered safe, it quickly became overcrowded with escaped slaves who thought their lives would be much improved within its walls. Instead, they found themselves subjected to, as a reporter for Frederick Douglass's newspaper, the *North Star*, reported, "brutal and cruel [treatment] to the extreme."

In 1862, cotton exporter Bernard Kock had secured a lease to a small Caribbean island, Île-à-Vache, off the coast of Haiti. Kock developed his own colonization effort to transport up to five thousand of the freed slaves at Fort Monroe to the uninhabited island, to begin a new life. Along with several influential backers, Kock presented his plan to Lincoln. After long negotiations, a contract was signed in which the US government would pay Kock $50 per emigrant to transport them to the island. The announcement of the project would coincide with Lincoln's signing of the Emancipation Proclamation.

There were several delays in implementing the contract, including rumors of Kock secretly making deals with the Confederacy to return the freed slaves back to the South once his ship set sail, causing Kock to be removed from the deal. Instead, a new contract was drawn up in which Kock would be kept on only because it was his island; the actual transport of the emigrants would be supervised by Charles K. Tuckerman and Paul M. Forbes, two men who were major backers of the project. The contract also limited the number of emigrants to only five hundred rather than the initially proposed five thousand.

On April 20, 1863, the vessel *Ocean Ranger* set a course for the island with 453 freedmen on board. The voyage and the Île-à-Vache project were doomed from the start. Three days out to sea, there was an outbreak of smallpox that quickly infected up to twenty passengers. Then, upon arriving at the island, Kock immediately declared himself governor, forcing the freedmen into signing contracts that basically made them Kock's slaves. Kock was also misappropriating funds that were meant to be used to construct housing for the newly freed slaves; instead, he used the money to build his own lavish house. When the ship arrived at the island, only two run-down huts had been completed, and there were barely enough supplies for the freedmen to make a go of it.

Weeks later, a US official went to visit the island, reporting back to the president that he found the settlers "with tears, misery, and sorrow in every countenance." A doctor who accompanied the official said the settlers were "beset by homesickness and depression of spirit."

By July 1864, Congress pulled funding for the project, and Lincoln never spoke of it again. The only mention of it came from Lincoln's personal secretary, John Hay, who wrote, "I am glad that the President has sloughed off that idea of colonization."

In our discussion of colonization, the terms "free Blacks" or "freedmen" have been used, which can be a bit confusing. While free Blacks were literally free to open their own businesses, worship freely, even offer their personal opinions publicly, it all boiled down to what part of the country they lived in. Being free still meant their lives were fraught with peril, and they faced danger from racist zealots. While the danger was more prevalent in the South, there was also a tinge of racism in Northern states as well.

For many free Blacks prior to and during the Civil War, living in an integrated society was a challenge. Southern plantation owners feared free Blacks, believing they were conspiring in barbershops and churches to organize slaves to revolt. It was also becoming increasingly evident that the practice of slavery was dying in the South, and would continue to die unless they won the war. Now, after the war, Whites were concerned about living side by side in an integrated society.

Several Southern state legislatures began drafting laws giving free Blacks two options: either leave that state altogether, preferably to their own country (colonization), or the state would basically confiscate their freedom and they would be sold into servitude. While these laws rarely passed, other legislation was enacted that would restrict free Blacks' movements in cities, with curfews and excessive taxes levied upon their businesses and wages.

By 1860, a new phenomenon was sweeping across the South: Free Blacks were submitting petitions to become slaves. Seeing that their lives were being degraded by new and tougher restrictions, and more importantly, because of the widespread fear they felt for their own lives and safety, many free Blacks started to believe their lives would be much better if they voluntarily signed themselves over to benevolent slaveholders.

You can read many of these tragic tales in the petitions submitted to local governments at archives across Southern states. They all read virtually the same, like one from a young woman in Alabama who requested the change in status because her husband had passed away. She was left destitute and "without protection." She was working as a servant for a wealthy doctor who apparently was kind to her, and as such, she believed she would be cared for and protected if she became his property.

Sometimes, a petition did not describe why the petitioner wanted to sign their lives away. Those simply say that the petitioner had requested to become the slave of (insert slave owner's name), "who is a person of good moral standing and proper person to become the master of the petitioner." Many of the documents are simply signed with an "X."

The practice of free Black men and women signing their lives into servitude became widespread enough that laws were established to regulate it. In many states, these regulations required that the "master-to-be" and the free African American declare their intentions (voluntarily becoming a slave), and that they verify the petition was submitted under the freeman's own free will. The local government would then have to guarantee that the petition would receive a hearing within ten days to make the request legal and binding. The slave owners were not permitted to acquire the new slave and then immediately sell them to pay off debts, and they had to pay a filing fee, usually $5, plus $15 for an attorney's fee.

With emancipation and the abolition of slavery in the United States following the Civil War, such practices became moot. However, a new and darker chapter was about to begin for Blacks in America, one of violent racism that lives on with us to this very day.

FOOTNOTE TO HISTORY: NANCE LEGINS-COSTLEY— THE FIRST FREED SLAVE

The "Great Emancipator," President Abraham Lincoln, freed millions of slaves from bondage, but what many people don't realize is that he had freed several slaves long before he became president. It happened while Lincoln was an attorney in Illinois, when the daughter of an indentured servant, Nance Legins-Costley, sued for her freedom. As her case was heading to the state Supreme Court, Lincoln became her lawyer.

Nance was born in 1813 in Kaskaskia, Illinois. The daughter of indentured servants, the young woman could also be held as a servant until the age of twenty-eight, even though the law in the state prohibited slavery. Slavery had been a part of the state before the Illinois constitution, and the law prohibiting slavery went into effect in 1818. Since the law was never fully enforced, the practice continued unabated.

Working in a hotel that housed prominent political and legal officials in the area, Nance, who was illiterate, learned about slave laws by listening in on the conversations between the lawyers. At fourteen, she was sold to another slave owner as a means of collecting the debt of her previous owner. That man, Colonel Tom Cox, sued to have his property—Nance Legins—returned. The case made it to the state Supreme Court, where his request was denied.

This is where things get complicated. The man who purchased Legins, Nathan Cromwell, was moving to Texas. He left Legins with a former business partner, David Bailey, but on his way to Texas, Cromwell died. Upon hearing the news, Nance Legins declared herself free.

In 1840, she married Benjamin Costley, but at about the same time, a relative of her former owner, Cromwell, sued his old business partner, David Bailey, for $400, and demanded that Nance Legins-Costley be returned. Bailey countered the suit, saying that the deal was nullified when Cromwell died. The Bailey and Legins-Costley case was heard by attorney Abraham Lincoln, who got to know the woman on a personal basis, a relationship that would help to forge the future president's antislavery position.

Lincoln took their case to the Illinois Supreme Court, and using the language of the state constitution that banned slavery, he argued that Legins-Costley's enslavement was unconstitutional—that, and the fact that she had been freed upon Cromwell's death.

The Supreme Court agreed, saying, "It is a presumption of law in the state of Illinois that every person is free without regard to color. The sale of a free person is illegal."

With her freedom secured, Nance Legins-Costley went on to fight for the right of other Blacks in the state, both free and enslaved. But this story has a sad ending. Nance passed away in 1893 at the age of seventy-nine, in Peoria, Illinois. She was buried in Peoria, but in 2017, the city relocated three thousand graves to a new location so that the area could be paved over. It was later found out that only one hundred graves were moved, while the rest were covered by asphalt.

Local residents installed a sign that lists the names of the forty-eight Union soldiers that remained buried on the site, but there are no records indicating whether Nance Legins-Costley's grave was one of those that were relocated, or if she is still buried in a modern tomb of pavement.

· 13 ·

THE LAST SLAVE SHIP:
THE *CLOTILDA*

B en Raines could be considered an environmental renaissance
man. Over the years, the journalist has won over two dozen
awards for his coverage of environmental issues on the Alabama
Gulf Coast. He has authored many books and articles on the subject and produced an award-winning documentary, *The Underwater
Forest*, which tells the story of a 70,000-year-old cypress forest recently discovered just off the coast in the Gulf of Mexico.

Ben has traveled and researched every backwater, bayou, and
slough in the 400-plus-square-mile Mobile–Tensaw River Delta,
the second-largest delta in the country that drains runoff from
much of the southeastern United States into the Gulf, making its
swamps and marshes rife with plant and aquatic life. During all of
those years paddling and boating in the delta, Ben was searching
for more than just an environmental story to feed to local and
national magazines and newspapers. He was also searching for a
legend, a historic artifact that researchers and historians had been
looking for over the past 160-plus years.

It was an artifact whose ghost loomed large over a community with its story of intrigue, despair, and, eventually, hope. No
one knew whether it was mere legend or the truth, but Ben knew

that finding evidence of it would provide an important link to a terrible time in American history, while at the same time offering closure and a source of pride for a community founded by those brought to America illegally as slaves on *Clotilda*, the last slave ship to arrive in the United States.

On April 9, 2018, after much research, Ben Raines donned his scuba gear and once again dove into the murky waters of the delta. When he surfaced, he held in his hand a small piece of wood. He had done it: He'd discovered the final resting place of the *Clotilda*. The search was over.

Researchers confirmed that Ben's find was indeed part of the slave ship, a sizable portion of its hull having been buried and preserved in the deep delta sediment. The fascinating story of how the vessel was able to smuggle 110 slaves from the country of Benin into the unforgiving dense, dangerous, and alligator-infested waters of the Mobile–Tensaw River Delta was not just a legend. Under cloak of darkness, the *Clotilda* made its way past American law enforcement agents and the US Navy, violating federal laws banning such ventures, in the end, leading to triumph when those she carried eventually earned their freedom and established the first town built and owned by former slaves.

Well before the United States officially became an independent country, European explorers who arrived to settle this New World had brought with them slaves captured in Africa and the West Indies, or they had enslaved Native Americans to do the backbreaking work of taming this untamed land. The first ship to bring captives to America arrived in Jamestown, Virginia, in August 1619. The Europeans felt justified in the practice because, as they believed, these people were "heathens," and as such, had no rights or freedoms and could be bought, sold, and traded as if they were property.

The common misconception is that all slaves brought to American shores were captured in their homeland and sailed into the United States to be sold at auction. Although this was true from the earliest days of the practice, it began to change during the Constitutional Convention of 1787, when convention delegates proposed outlawing the importation of slaves into the country by the year 1808. The proposed law was mentioned by President Thomas Jefferson in his December 1806 letter to both the US House of Representatives and the US Senate (a written version of a State of the Union address). In the letter, Jefferson encouraged Congress to pass the proposed law:

I congratulate you, fellow Citizens, on the approach of the period at which you may interpose your authority Constitutionally, to withdraw the citizens of the United States from all further participation in those violations of human rights, which have been so long continued on the unoffending Inhabitants of Africa, and which the morality, the reputation, & the best interests of our country have long been eager to proscribe. Although no law you may pass can take prohibitory effect till the first day of the year one thousand eight hundred & eight, yet the intervening period is not too long to prevent, by timely notice, expeditions which cannot be completed before that day.

And that they did. On March 7, 1807, the Act Prohibiting the Importation of Slaves was passed into law, and on January 1, 1808, it became illegal to import slaves into the United States. This did not mean that the institution of slavery had ended. On the contrary. It just meant that new slaves could not be imported into the United States from foreign countries.

At the same time, an economic boom was growing in the South, literally—cotton. Many enterprising businessmen from the North saw this as an opportunity to cash in on the prosperity and began flocking into the South, bringing with them many more Blacks to be used as slaves. Even with the new law, the slave trade continued unabated, with enslaved men, women, and children being shipped into the South and then traded or sold in the shadows.

Many times if a ship was caught violating the law with a cargo of captured Blacks, the boat would be seized, but the captured passengers were still allowed to be sold. Such was the case with the schooners *Constitution*, *Merino*, and *Louisa* in 1825. The vessels were captured, and their captains convicted of violating the Act Prohibiting the Importation of Slaves, but the ship's captured passengers were eventually sold, with all proceeds being turned over to the court.

Four years earlier, another ship, the *Ohio*, was seized by the government, who found two female slaves on board. The boat was heading from New Orleans to Philadelphia. The law only dealt with the international slave trade, not interstate, and nothing came of the ship's seizure. So, as you see, while the law was well meaning, it did nothing to squelch slavery in the United States.

For the most part, the 1808 law was successful in stopping the importation of slaves into the United States, as an article in the November 17, 1862, edition of the *New York Times* described:

> *We have the names of over one hundred and fifty vessels which were engaged in the trade from 1858 to 1861. . . . Of this number, thirty-eight were seized on the coast of Africa . . . and over thirteen thousand negroes were returned to Africa. A correspondent high in official standing writing from Havana stated the fact that upward of thirty thousand Africans had been landed on the island during the single year previous.*

The article continued with a detailed list in date order of all the ships that had either been seized out at sea and the captured African cargo returned to their homeland, or had been forced by British or US naval vessels to turn around and head back to whence they came. The list proved that at least when it came to importing slaves, the law was actually working—that is, until you came to the entry dated July 10, 1860, which simply read:

"The schooner *Clotilda* landed a cargo of negroes at Mobile. No arrests were made."

The voyage of the *Clotilda* had begun on a bet. Just prior to the Civil War, the demand for slave labor in the South was at an all-time high. The term "Cotton is king" was not an exaggeration. The entire Southern economy was based on the crop, and profits for plantation owners were soaring. Plantations were unable to keep up with demand, since they relied solely on slave labor to handle the backbreaking work of tilling new land, planting the fields, and then harvesting the crop. The owners' ability to import new slaves had been taken away with the law, and the migration to the South of Northerners who brought their own slaves with them had come to a halt. But then plantation owner and shipbuilder Timothy Meaher made a wager.

As with many Northerners, the Maine-born Meaher moved to Mobile around 1830 and opened what would become a highly profitable shipbuilding business where he built steamboats that would ferry goods and people from Mobile to Montgomery, Alabama. Sometime in the late 1850s, Meaher was with a few friends aboard the steamboat *Roger B. Taney*, chatting casually and having a few drinks. That night, he made a wager with the guests. According to accounts by those in attendance, Meaher said, "I bet a thousand dollars that inside two years, I myself can bring a ship full of n****** into Mobile Bay under the officers' noses." Everyone in attendance was confident that Meaher couldn't pull off the move, and they took the bet.

Meaher went to work to make sure he won the wager. First, he hired a captain to pilot the ship to Africa. His choice was a close friend of his, thirty-seven-year-old William Foster. Foster was also a shipbuilder and had constructed an 86-foot, two-masted schooner, the *Clotilda*, which Meaher purchased for $35,000. The boat was designed more for river operations or nearshore Gulf voyages, not a transatlantic trip, so Meaher made significant modifications to the boat, making it sail lower in the water and adding larger masts that could accommodate broad sails, all in an effort to make it a swift racer that would be able to outrun any ship on the sea.

Next, Meaher needed to assemble a crew, but many of the men he approached declined the job due to its illegality. They knew that if the ship were caught by either the US or British Navy, they would either face jail time or be left stranded in Africa, or on some remote island near where the ship was seized, with no way of getting home. The crew Meaher eventually signed on did so without being told what they had signed up for.

On March 3, 1860, the *Clotilda* set sail for Africa, evading patrol ships just off the Alabama coast. On March 17, the ship was caught in a violent, almost voyage-ending storm while being pursued by a Portuguese man-of-war. On April 14, as the *Clotilda* neared Cabo Verde islands, another Portuguese ship began pursuit. Captain Foster was able to outmaneuver the ship and escape capture.

As the *Clotilda* neared the port city of Ouidah in the Kingdom of Dahomey (now known as Benin), the crew was told about the true mission of the ship. They threatened to mutiny, only acquiescing when Meaher offered them double their salary when they returned to Mobile.

For decades, the Kingdom of Dahomey had been at war in one way or another, either with its neighbors, or with itself, in a bloody civil war. At the time of the *Clotilda*'s arrival, many warriors and civilians had been imprisoned in a slave pen called a "barracoon." From this group, Meaher selected 110 of the prisoners to be slaves, and then began the return trip home.

Meanwhile, back in the United States, federal authorities had intercepted word of Meaher's bet and were keeping a close eye on the Alabama Gulf coast, waiting for the ship's return. On July 9, 1860, when darkness fell, the *Clotilda* silently sailed back into

Mobile Bay, right under the noses of the federal patrols. The ship sailed up into the delta where it was met by a riverboat. Captain Foster transferred the captives to the riverboat and sent it further north into the backwaters, where the captured Africans would disembark into the alligator-infested swamp and spend the night in a temporary camp.

In the meantime, Foster and Meaher grounded the *Clotilda* along the banks of a canal and set it on fire to hide the evidence. The burnt-out hulk of the ship eventually sank into the thick sediment of the river, not to be seen again for 160 years.

The captives were divided into two groups, one under the control of Meaher, the other with Foster, and they were kept as slaves for the next five years. The following year, after the *Clotilda* had returned to Mobile, Meaher was arrested and put on trial by the federal government for defying the 1808 act prohibiting the transport of slaves into the United States. Either because of a lack of evidence (the ship had been destroyed) or the fact that the Civil War had begun, the case was dismissed.

Five years after the *Clotilda* returned to Mobile, the Civil War was over and slavery had been abolished. The captured Africans from the *Clotilda* were set free. Not having enough money to return to Africa, a group of the freed men and women pooled what money they did have, earned from growing vegetables and working the fields, to purchase a few acres of land from the man who had brought them to America in the first place, Timothy Meaher. On that land, they created a unique community, the only one completely built and governed by former slaves: Africatown.

Until Ben Raines's discovery in 2018 of that single charred piece of wood, the story of the *Clotilda* had been treated as myth. But for the hundreds of descendants of the men and women who were brought to these shores and still live in Africatown to this day, it was always more than just a legend. The discovery of the ship completed their history that had eluded them for over a century.

The discovery of the *Clotilda* brought together the descendants of the former slaves with descendants of Timothy Meaher—not to relive the past, but to make an effort to understand it, along with their shared history.

Further exploration of the wreck site reveals that a considerable amount of the ship has been preserved under the sediment. Plans are being considered to try and raise the *Clotilda*, or at least to create a monument, perhaps like the USS *Arizona* memorial at Pearl Harbor, to commemorate this important piece of American history, an incredible legacy the descendants of the last slave ship to arrive in America can be proud to share with the world.

FOOTNOTE TO HISTORY: FREEDOM TOWNS

While the story of the *Clotilda* and the creation of Africatown is fascinating, it is important to remember that Africatown was not the first town (also known as Freedom Towns or Black Towns) built by, and for, freed slaves. The first we know of was the town of Gracia Real de Santa Teresa de Mose, 2 miles north of present-day St. Augustine, Florida. Although it wasn't the first such town in the British colonies that would become the United States, it was still the first in the New World.

In what could be considered the first Underground Railroad, escaped slaves from the colonies would be shuttled south into Spanish-held Florida. The first group—eight men, two women, and a three-year-old child—arrived in St. Augustine in 1687, where the governor of the town granted them asylum. More followed, and with a promise of loyalty to the King of Spain and their conversion to the Catholic faith, the former slaves were provided their own sanctuary, the fortified village of Mose, in 1738.

These Freedom Towns began popping up across the South immediately following the Civil War. Much like those brought to the United States on the *Clotilda*, freed slaves would use what little money they could earn by selling fruits and vegetables grown on their own small plots of land to purchase acreage where homes and businesses could be built, and they could begin a new life in a free community that they governed.

Other Freedom Towns of note include the 200 acres of farmland known as Sugarland, Maryland, a town built only 20 miles north of Washington, DC. The deed for the land called for the town to be "a place of excellence for persons of African descent." The farming town had stores, homes, and a church that still stands today. Just east of Birmingham, Alabama, is the town of Hobson City (formerly Mooree Quarters) that was founded in 1899 and is the first incorporated Black city in the state. And prior to the Civil War, in Brooklyn, New York, the town of Weeksville was established by a former slave, James Week. Today it is known as Crown Heights / Bedford Stuyvesant. Between 1865 and 1915, over sixty Black towns were created in all regions of the country.

· 14 ·

CATFISHING BEFORE IT WAS
A THING: THE STORY
OF FLOSSIE LEE

It has always been fascinating to me how a common English word transforms over the years to take on a new meaning. For example, it wasn't long ago that every business office had a Xerox copier in their building, and if you wanted to make a copy, you would say, "I need to have this Xeroxed." Today, no matter what brand of copy machine your office has, or even if you take a document to Staples or Office Depot, many people still say they have to have it Xeroxed.

There are countless other examples of how everyday words have taken on a new meaning over the centuries, like "catfishing," for example. For some, this calls up the image of a lone figure on the banks of a river, cane pole in hand, wetting the line to try and catch a huge river catfish. In the world of the Internet and social media, however, it's taken on a new and darker connotation. Although you may believe it's a relatively new phenomenon that began in 2010, with the release of a documentary film, the practice of "catfishing" innocent people began decades earlier, long before the idea of interconnected computers and worldwide chat sites were even thought of.

We will come to that in a moment, but first, we need to know what catfishing has become to understand the past. The act of catfishing in modern terms deals with a person taking on a fake identity, a fictious online persona, with every intention of deceiving, harassing, or scamming others. A person may do this for many reasons, one of which was the focus of *Catfish*, a 2010 documentary produced by Henry Joost and Ariel Schulman. The filmmakers had watched as a story unfolded before their eyes, involving Schulman's brother, Nev. They thought it would make for a gripping movie, one that IMDb calls "a reality thriller that is a shocking product of our times," and one where the term "catfishing" first took on its new meaning. (Spoiler alert, if you haven't seen the film.)

The story follows New York photographer Nev who has been posting his photographs online, and begins chatting with eight-year-old Abby. Abby is an admirer of his work and writes to him to let him know she's been following him on his social media site. Abby claims to be a painter, and wants Nev's permission to recreate one of his photos as a painting. He agrees, and from then on, the two begin chatting more, soon becoming close online friends. The next thing Nev knows, he finds himself chatting with Abby's mother and her nineteen-year-old sister, Megan.

Nev begins to feel an attraction to Megan, and after eight months of flirting with her online, Nev believes he has fallen in love with her. He decides it's time for the two of them to meet in person, and makes plans to head to Michigan to meet her face-to-face. The person he finds isn't who he expected. (Here's where the spoiler alert comes in.)

Megan—and, in fact, Abby, as well as all of Abby's "relatives"—were actually one person: Angela Wesselman-Pierce, a middle-aged artist whose paintings had been rejected and ridiculed by other artists and random people online. Looking for validation, Angela had set up the fake persona of Abby as well as the other family members by creating multiple Myspace accounts under the fictitious family names. She even went so far as to curate and post fake photos of the family. The scheme worked, attracting one caring soul, Nev, who befriended her. Angela did send Nev her actual paintings, but when Nev called her to set up the meeting, she had her voice manipulated over the phone to fool him.

Besides the shunning and ridicule of others online, Angela had been isolated from the world. Her disappointed ambitions went far beyond the ridicule she experienced online; her dreams had also been thwarted by life itself. Angela was married, but her entire life revolved around nonstop caring for her husband's two disabled sons. The exaggerated personas she created gave her freedom and a means of escaping everyday life.

At the end of the movie, the word for this type of behavior is coined by Angela's husband:

> *They used to tank cod from Alaska all the way to China. They'd keep them in vats in the ship. By the time the codfish reached China, the flesh was mush and tasteless. So this guy came up with the idea that if you put these cods in these big vats [and] put some catfish in with them, the catfish will keep the cod agile. And there are those people who are catfish in life. And they keep you on your toes. They keep you guessing, they keep you thinking, they keep you fresh. And I thank God for the catfish, because we would be boring and dull if we didn't have somebody nipping at our fins.*

With that, the act of creating a fake persona to deceive, manipulate, or scam a person online became known as "catfishing."

As you can see, Angela's tale is a sad one of a lonely person trapped in a life she couldn't escape. Her alter ego gave her the means to live another life, even if only a fictitious one. But there are many other reasons why people resort to catfishing. Many of the "expeditions" are for more than just social interaction; some are devious plots designed to smear another person's good name, even blackmail them and extort money. Many times, sex is used as the bait in what is called "sextortion." One of the most common forms of sextortion is for a person to pose as a young woman or man, hooking an online victim into a conversation which eventually turns into a flirtation that develops into a pseudo-romance. Before long, sex enters the equation, and the person who instigated the chats begins talking about having erotic adventures with the victim, eventually asking for explicit photographs. Once the instigator of the conversation receives the photos, their true motives are revealed: They divulge that their identity is made up and the blackmailing for money begins.

Catfishing has actually been around for quite a while, long before the advent of the Internet and the movie *Catfish*, although it wasn't called that at the time, and it was done through newspapers rather than online. One catfishing scam that most closely resembles today's version dates back to 1890. It is the story of a Miss Flossie Lee and how the government tracked "her" down and put an end to Flossie's catfishing scheme.

The story actually begins years earlier, during the Civil War, when a young Union soldier, Anthony Comstock, was appalled at the behavior of his comrades, including their excessive use of alcohol and tobacco, their fondness for gambling and foul language, and their possession of lewd and obscene material that was being freely distributed to the men by various publishers at the time. Comstock was brought up in a religious home where his mother held strict moral beliefs, which she instilled in her son. To Comstock, such vices were the product of the devil and needed to be vanquished.

Prior to his enlistment in the army, Comstock attempted to have a saloon in his hometown shut down for serving drinks on Sunday. When the local sheriff ignored his complaints, Comstock took the matter into his own hands and destroyed all of the saloon's barrels of alcohol. Needless to say, the behavior he saw in the military was simply abhorrent. In the army, Comstock took it upon himself to fight "the good fight," becoming a member of the Christian Commission, an organization formed by the Young Men's Christian Association (YMCA) that sent ministers to battlefields in an attempt to instill good morals in the troops.

Upon his discharge, Comstock moved to New York City where his senses and moral values were assaulted by the amount of readily available pornography, prostitution, contraceptives, and abortion services. Contraceptives, in his opinion, were the root of all evil, since they permitted lust and free sex.

Incensed with what he saw, Comstock crafted his own piece of legislation that would make it illegal to send "obscene, lewd, or lascivious, immoral or indecent publications through the mail." The term *obscenity* was not outlined in the proposed law, and as such, was open to all manner of interpretations.

Comstock took his proposed bill to Washington, presented it to congressmen, and on March 3, 1873, the Comstock Act was enacted. With its passage, Comstock was designated a special agent to the US Post Office and was given the power to enact the law and arrest individuals he believed to have violated its provisions. He wished to restrict far more than simple pornography—educational material on precautions to follow for safe sex, and even medical textbooks on female reproductive health were in his sights. Ads for all such material quickly disappeared from publications. Well, actually, they didn't disappear. They were "rebranded." The new advertisements offered "artists" a series of photographs of beautiful women that they could use as inspiration to create paintings and sculptures.

Fast-forward fifteen years to the town of Augusta, Maine, where a small photography business, the Art Photo Company, appeared to be doing quite well for itself. According to the National Archives office in Boston, the "proprietor," Miss Flossie Lee, was selling "artistic" photos, legally, for $1. As long as they were sold as being for artistic purposes, the sales and mailing of the photos were legitimate.

Business at the Art Photo Company was booming, which brought it to the attention of the US Postal Service. They believed the company was selling full-blown pornographic books, not just artistic photos to a local audience, but up to this point, hadn't been able to prove it, so it was pushed to the back burner.

That all changed in January of 1890, when the company decided to expand and take its business nationwide. Their first advertisement appeared in the January 1890 edition of the national crime magazine, the *National Police Gazette*. The ad began with a big, bold, attention-grabbing headline that shouted, "My Own Photo," then continued:

> *I am the acknowledged beau of my own city and have beaux by the score, but wish to extend my acquaintance over the whole country. I will send a large cabinet photo of my own beautiful self with my autograph. Besides, I will I put in one dozen (12) photos, on Full Cabinet-Size Cards, of charming young lady friends, sweet, bewitching girls, making in all 13 Exquisite Pictures for 25c., silver.*

The ad ended with the name Miss Flossie Lee, and her address: c/o Box 3, Station 101, Augusta, Maine. It was quite obvious this was an outright advertisement for pornographic photos, and as it turned out, it became one of the first pornographic subscription services. After sending the initial 25 cents, patrons could subscribe and receive regular photos from Flossie Lee and her friends.

The photos were nowhere near as explicit as they are today, portraying youthful women posing in their "unmentionables." No nudity was involved, but that didn't matter. The ad was a success, and money began flowing in, mostly from sixteen-year-old boys. Of course, while young boys have a knack of hiding things like this from their parents, the parents would ultimately find the material stashed away in their sons' rooms. All across the country, law enforcement agencies and post offices were being deluged with letters from outraged parents, demanding that Flossie Lee be shut down.

The complaints eventually made their way to Washington and the offices of senators and congressmen. Congressman Henry Clay McCormick ordered an investigation into Flossie Lee's business with the goal of shutting her down, but with only a post office box, they had little information to go on.

In late 1890, Boston postal inspector Charles Pendleton, using an alias of his own, Eugene Boon, placed an order with Flossie Lee. On December 12, his package arrived: a complete set of risqué photographs. Pendleton now had evidence in hand as to what type of business Flossie Lee was actually running. The Art Photo Company might never have been discovered as the perpetrator, or at least stayed in business for much longer, except for the fact that the company's name and address was stamped on the back of the sheet of thirteen images.

Pendleton received another important clue as to who was behind the business when he took a closer look at the postal receipt that accompanied the images. As it turned out, Flossie Lee was not a real person. The whole thing was a catfishing scheme being perpetrated by someone with the name of "George Dunton," one of the signatures he'd noticed on the receipt.

Dunton was a well-known and extremely popular citizen of Augusta, having designed a new method of electrotyping text and images in publications for his employer, E. C. Allen Publishing. Dunton had decided to create his own side business, the Art Photo Company, in 1888. Originally, he had purchased illegal photographs from distributors in New York City who obtained their stock from European dealers. Dunton would reprint and resell the material through his subscription service for the price of $1. His source for images dried up after a fire in one of the dealers' warehouses had destroyed all of the material, but Dunton had retained the negatives for many of the photos, and began printing and selling them as the Flossie Lee collection, for a quarter.

In the fall of 1891, under the advisement of his lawyers, Dunton halted operations, but it was too late, and he was arrested by federal agents. His lawyers told the court that Dunton was unaware that what he was doing was illegal. At the end of his trial, the judge noted that if Dunton had continued selling the material as "art," he would have gotten away with it. The judge said that the Flossie Lee material was obviously of a sexual nature, and thus a violation of the Comstock Act. In addition, the fact that Flossie Lee was a fictious character also made the case for mail fraud. Dunton was sentenced to four months in jail.

Upon his release, Dunton continued in the electrotyping business, now in Washington, DC, where he published several popular engineering booklets on electrotyping before passing away in 1916, at the age of fifty-five. Little did Dunton realize that his Flossie Lee scam would be a forerunner of a worldwide, highly illegal, and unscrupulous business model called "catfishing."

FOOTNOTE TO HISTORY: AERIAL NEWSBOYS

Gone are the days when a kid's first job would be that of a paperboy (or -girl), riding their bikes around the neighborhood and delivering the morning newspaper door to door. With amazing skill and dexterity, they would fling the paper on target, landing it on the front doorstep, all while whizzing down the street and guiding their bike with one hand. Well, landing the paper on the doorstep was the goal, even though it didn't always happen, sometimes landing in the bushes or on a roof. Still, it was quite a feat.

Now imagine throwing newspapers from an airplane to a target on the ground. That would be quite the daunting task, landing a stack of newspapers on the mark without hitting a person or damaging a roof. Making it even more difficult would be the speed the papers would gain by the time they hit the ground, or an unsuspecting passerby. Doing the math, if a stack of newspapers were dropped from 500 feet, the papers would hit the ground at 122 mph. Lowering the altitude to 100 feet in the air, they would still crash down at 55 mph.

Those figures, while daunting, didn't stop newspaperman Harry Strunk. The founder of the *Red Willow County* (Nebraska) *Gazette* produced many ideas to boost sales of his newspapers. Each year he would offer a brand-new car to the top three salesmen in his circulation and sales departments. The *Gazette*'s office building became one of the first locations in the country that collected toys at Christmas to be distributed to families in need. And then he came up with the unique, attention-grabbing idea of delivering newspapers by airplane. Not door to door, but as major distribution drops, where (if they survived the fall) the stack would then be delivered to homes throughout the area.

The first to experiment with the paper drop was the *Detroit News*. Pilot Ted Fordon took to the skies with copies of the *News* on July 26, 1919, in a rickety

Curtiss "Jenny" JN-4 aircraft. The concept was good, but unsuccessful for the Detroit publisher.

The idea finally took hold ten years later when Strunk purchased a two-seat Curtiss Robin C-1 plane that he called the *Newsboy* and flew over Kansas City, mapping out a route where his pilot, Steve Tuttle, could start dropping about five thousand copies of the *McCook Daily Gazette* Monday through Saturday. Strunk modified the plane by removing the passenger seat and cutting a hole in the floor. He then added a chute and a trapdoor. The idea was to place a stack of papers on the trapdoor and then open it by activating a lever. Tuttle's brother George would ride along and load the chute with bundles of newspapers; when given the signal, he would open the trapdoor and the papers would drop out of the plane. They landed in a field—the property owner had given Strunk permission to use it for the drops—and the papers were then picked up and delivered to houses across town.

The idea was a hit; towns big and small could now receive the newspaper daily, within hours after it was printed. As Strunk declared before the inaugural flight, "No home is more than two hours from the press." Sadly, the age of airplane newspaper drops was not long for this world; costs skyrocketed as the Great Depression set in, and that was the end of aerial newspaper delivery.

· 15 ·

WHEN THE "NOBLE EXPERIMENT" TURNED DEADLY

Twenty years before the enactment of the Eighteenth Amendment to the Constitution in 1909 that banned the manufacture, sale, and transport of alcoholic beverages, a small independent publisher, the Lincoln Temperance Press, published its annual *American Prohibition Yearbook*. Like many such books of its kind published at the beginning of the twentieth century by other independent and university presses, the book began with an uplifting message for those in the temperance movement:

> *Prohibition wins its way to the hearts of the people. It becomes a part of manly and womanly purpose. Liquor men for four years have prophesized that the wave of prohibition would subside. It has not subsided . . . Notwithstanding the fierce contests of the past year, total abstinence has strengthened its hold upon the mind and conscience of the people.*

Indeed, the temperance movement—a movement dedicated to restricting or abolishing the consumption of liquor and alcoholic drinks across the country, and if possible, the world—had been making inroads toward convincing people of the evils of the "demon drink." But even with the movement's slow but steady progress, the consumption of alcohol continued virtually unabated, even after the Eighteenth Amendment was passed. Despite the goal of the amendment, Americans still wanted their drink.

Little did the public realize that the least of their worries would be overconsumption. Their drinking habits would become even more deadly when they found themselves being poisoned by their own government.

For centuries, the consumption of alcohol was believed to be beneficial to one's health, thought to aid in pain relief, fighting fatigue, and warding off "the fever." Europeans first arriving in the New World brought with them the ingredients to make liquor and soon began manufacturing their own alcoholic beverages, calling them a blessing. They would drink wine for breakfast, take breaks from work for a sip at eleven a.m. and four p.m., and then partake in cider, beer, and other hard beverages at dinner and just before bedtime.

Alcohol wasn't just a "healthy" option for the colonists but also a form of revenue, with ad valorem taxes being levied on imported wines and spirits, the proceeds going to build schools, prisons, and more.

While readily available and routinely consumed, excessive alcoholism was condemned and punished as an abuse of the "God-given gift." Early in American history, limitations on the hours of operation for taverns was imposed, laws against serving slaves were introduced, taverns were required to provide lodging and food for those who'd had a few too many, and in some cases, fines were levied against drunks. Even whippings were known to be a form of punishment for public drunkenness.

Benjamin Rush, an advisor to President Thomas Jefferson, published a contrary view of alcohol in 1785. He believed that people did not need to drink to be healthy. In fact, they were actually poisoning themselves. By 1800, however, alcohol consumption was skyrocketing. It is estimated that the annual per capita consumption of hard alcohol had risen from 2.5 gallons to 10 gallons per person. And that was a conservative estimate.

A group of farmers in Moreau and North Cumberland, New York, formed the first organized temperance movement in 1808, inspired by Benjamin Rush: the Union Temperance Society. The fledgling movement increased in size exponentially over the next few years, boasting over 13 million members by 1835. Even future president Abraham Lincoln saw what good could come from the movement during a speech he gave to the Second Presbyterian Church in Springfield, Illinois, on February 22, 1842, the 110th anniversary of George Washington's birthday. In his speech, Lincoln chastised previous harsh attempts at converting people away from drinking, instead believing that compassion was the right course of action:

> *Although the Temperance cause has been in progress for near twenty years, it is apparent to all, that it is, just now, being crowned with a degree of success, hitherto unparalleled. . . . In it, we shall find a stronger bondage broken; a viler slavery, manumitted; a greater tyrant deposed. In it, more of want supplied, more disease healed, more sorrow assuaged. By it no orphans starving, no widows weeping.*

As the twentieth century began, the movement was gaining momentum, and in 1916, twenty-three states passed laws that put heavy restrictions on saloons and the selling of alcohol. One year later, the US Senate took up the issue and passed a proposed constitutional amendment that would nationally ban the manufacture, sale, distribution, and transportation of alcohol. With slight modifications, the House of Representatives passed the bill, and it was sent out for a vote by the people. In late 1918, the bill was officially ratified by the states, and on January 16, 1919, the Eighteenth Amendment to the Constitution was ratified in Washington, effectively making the United States a "dry" country one year later. That is, almost dry.

The new amendment had a few flaws, the most notable of which is that it did not provide for enforcement of the new law. An attempt was made by Congress to correct that omission by passing the National Prohibition Act, also known as the Volstead Act, only months prior to the Eighteenth Amendment taking effect. With the passage of the law and the Eighteenth Amendment going into effect, initial consumption of alcohol decreased dramatically, but it didn't take long before the working class began drinking more at home, at "athletic" clubs, and at illegal saloons, better known as speakeasies.

Bootlegging ran rampant and brought a new entrepreneur to the forefront—gangsters. Mob-run bootlegging operations saw incredible profits as they skirted the law, producing and stealthily importing alcohol into the United States. One of the most famous mob bosses of the time, Al Capone, lamented: "When I sell liquor, it's bootlegging. When my patrons serve it on a silver tray on [Chicago's] Lake Shore Drive, it's hospitality."

Despite frequent raids and the destruction of thousands of barrels of alcohol by the federal agents, bootlegging in one form or another was incredibly lucrative. In 1926, the government estimated that the sale of illegal liquor amounted to a net profit of $3.6 billion for the mob. One of the few loopholes the Volstead Act left open was an exemption for alcohol used in religious services, such as sacramental wine. The Federal Council of Churches reported in 1926 that "there is no way of knowing what the legitimate consumption of fermented sacramental wine is, but it is clear that the legitimate demand does not increase by 800,000 gallons in two years."

The Volstead Act also provided that alcohol used for medicinal purposes was exempt, even though prior to its enactment, the

American Medical Association had decreed that alcohol was of no medicinal use. The act did require doctors to apply for a special permit before prescribing such medicine, and that the prescription had to have been manufactured in government-approved distilleries. Doctors and pharmacists were suddenly making a fortune. In Chicago, Walgreens went from having only twenty-five drugstores in the city to over five hundred nationwide.

The problem with illegal alcohol (sometimes called "rotgut") was that it often had an obnoxious odor and taste. To mask the unpleasant aroma and taste, bootleggers would often add flavorings, including ginger extract. Unfortunately, the additive masked more than just the taste. It also led to an outbreak of what was called "jake leg," or "ginger jake paralysis," caused by using improperly manufactured ginger extract. The extract contained a neurotoxin called tri-ortho-cresyl phosphate, or TOCP. If enough was ingested, the toxin caused severe nerve damage, muscle weakness, numbness, and even paralysis. The main source of ginger extract came from a Boston distillery, Boston Hub Products. In the end, between 50,000 and 100,000 people were crippled by the drink that the company marketed as Jamaica Ginger. And while the ingredients were not illegal, the company's owners were fined $1,000 each and received a two-year suspended jail sentence. Families of those afflicted with jake leg received no compensation.

At the same time, production of industrial alcohol—also known as grain alcohol or denatured alcohol (ethanol), used in factories as a cleaning solvent—was exempt from the new law and continued to be manufactured in great quantities, just as it had been prior to Prohibition. The difference was, now it became a prime target for bootleggers, who would steal the alcohol and resell it as drink. In 1925, the estimate was that over 60 million gallons of industrial alcohol had been stolen. Something had to be done to stop the thefts and in turn, the devastating effects it was having on the public.

Enter the US Treasury Department. In 1926, President Calvin Coolidge ordered that chemicals be added to the alcohol to deter drinking the product. Many companies added the poisonous methyl alcohol, but in true entrepreneurial style, the clever bootleggers concocted methods of "renaturing" the denatured alcohol. In response, the federal government ordered even more and deadlier formulas to be introduced into the alcohol's production. Soon, gasoline, cadmium, iodine, nicotine, formaldehyde, chloroform, kerosene, and even a relative of the strychnine family, brucine, was added to manufactured industrial alcohol.

The effects devastated populations across the country in what amounted to the mandated poisoning of Americans by the government. In New York City on Christmas Eve, 1926, it was reported that a man flushed with fear ran into Bellevue Hospital screaming hysterically that Santa Claus was going to attack him with a bat. Soon after arriving, the man fell to the floor and died in the lobby. Before long, the hospital was overrun with patients, at least sixty, who had fallen ill, with eight of those dying that night. The cause: drinking tainted alcohol.

Until that horrible Christmas Eve in 1926, only 1,200 New Yorkers had been sickened and 400 had died from the additives. Not a trivial number by any means, but after the government upped the ante with harsher additives, the number rose to 700 dead the following year. Those numbers were duplicated in cities across the country.

The New York City medical examiner, Dr. Charles Norris, quickly assembled a press conference to chastise the federal government's orders to use additives:

[The government] continues its poisoning processes, heedless of the fact that the people determined to drink are daily absorbing that poison. Knowing this to be true, the United States government must

be charged with the moral responsibility for the deaths that poisoned liquor causes, although it cannot be held legally responsible.

Norris went on to publicize all alcohol-related deaths in newspapers and issued several blunt warnings to city dwellers, telling them that "practically all the liquor that is sold in New York today is toxic." One New York assemblyman named Phelps told the *New York Times* that "[this] isn't death by accident. It was wholesale murder by design."

The practice of putting additives in alcohol continued up until the Eighteenth Amendment was repealed on December 5, 1933. For the most part, bootlegging operations ceased, saloons and taverns reopened, and the federal government quietly and without fanfare halted the requirement placed on industrial alcohol manufacturers to put poisonous additives into their product.

FOOTNOTE TO HISTORY: THE TRUTH ABOUT SPEAKEASIES

When we think of a speakeasy, we can't help but think of all of those glorious black-and-white mobster movies that depict the Prohibition Era. The typical scene shows a lone figure knocking on an ominous-looking door. A small slit in the door is covered by a narrow sliding cover, the opening just wide enough to reveal two menacing eyes glaring at them. Once the "eyes" give the person a once-over, one of two things happens: either a voice asks for a password, or the person knocking tells the one guarding the door, "Johnny sent me," or the like. The door opens and the person is admitted into the joint, where illegal alcohol—some authentic, some tainted—is flowing, music is blaring, dancers are packing the floor.

When discussing Prohibition, it is a common mistake to think that speakeasies began as soon as alcohol sales and distribution became illegal in the United States, but in fact, the term and its connection to alcohol was first used in print in 1909. Journalist Samuel Hudson wrote in his book, *Pennsylvania and Its Public Men*, about a strict liquor law that was passed in Pittsburgh in 1889 that greatly reduced the number of taverns and saloons in the city. The result was the opening of illegal bars across the town. When Hudson visited one of these bars, he was told that an elderly Irish woman who owned one of the bars would warn her patrons to beware of the police and not to spill the beans about the illegal bar's activities. "Spake asy," she said in a deep Irish brogue. "The police are at the dure."

Hearing the story, Hudson rushed back to his home base in Philadelphia to write an article for a local newspaper about these "speakeasies." The term caught on for any illegal bar that popped up, and when Prohibition rolled around in 1919, the term was resurrected for the thousands of illegal bars that sprang up nationwide.

Entrances to speakeasies were always kept secret, for obvious reasons. They could be behind a staircase, a door hidden behind bookshelves, but mainly, those large, imposing doors. According to the Mob Museum in Las Vegas, the doors were most often painted a specific color to identify them as an entrance to a speakeasy—for example, in Chicago, the doors were painted green. The museum shares a story of one of these green doors in Chicago, concerning "Machine Gun" Jack McGurn, a partner of Al Capone's. When McGurn requested that comedian Joe E. Lewis perform at his Green Mill Club in 1927, Lewis refused, and McGurn decided that Lewis needed to pay a price. Sending three men to Lewis's home, they slit his throat and face. Lewis survived the incident, but only thanks to mob leader Al Capone, who paid for his medical expenses.

· 16 ·

The "First" Female US President

Over the course of American history, there is one glass ceiling that still hasn't been broken . . . yet: inaugurating the first woman president. Several women have made a run for the office, with Hillary Rodham Clinton and Kamala Harris coming the closest to breaking that ceiling during the 2016 and 2024 elections, respectively. Kamala Harris did achieve the second highest position in the US government, that of vice president, with the election of Joe Biden as president in 2020. Many historians, however, argue that we have already had a woman president.

Woodrow Wilson was born the son of a pastor in Augusta, Georgia. Prior to being elected president, Wilson earned his law degree at Princeton College in New Jersey and the University of Virginia Law School before earning a doctorate at Johns Hopkins University. Conservative Democrats urged him to run for the governorship of New Jersey in 1910, which he did, and won, but once in office, he quickly turned away from a conservative philosophy to a more liberal one, seeing the role of governor, or any high-ranking political office, as being one where the occupant should work tirelessly as a personal representative of the people.

When Wilson was only six years old, he unknowingly met his first wife when his family visited Rome, Georgia. Ellen Louise Axson was only a baby at the time, but by 1883, as a fledgling lawyer, Wilson met Axson again. She was now a refined young woman described as calm, sweet, and motherly. When Wilson was reintroduced to her, he commented, "What splendid laughing eyes!" It was love at first sight, and the two married in 1885, eventually having three children together.

When Wilson was elected president in 1913, Ellen took on the role of first lady with dignity and grace, although she admitted to Wilson's predecessor, President William Howard Taft, "I am naturally the most unambitious of women, and life in the White House has no attraction for me." Being the granddaughter of a former slaveholder, as first lady Ellen took it upon herself to advocate for better housing in the Black community surrounding the nation's capital.

One year after entering the White House, Ellen became extremely ill and was diagnosed with Bright's disease, which causes the body's immune system to attack the lungs and liver. On August 6, 1914, the first lady succumbed to the disease. Wilson went into a deep depression. Ellen's casket was placed inside a train's baggage car for burial in her hometown of Rome, Georgia. The president rode the entire long journey in the baggage car alongside his wife. It was only later that Wilson's personal physician, Dr. Cary Grayson, told Wilson that his wife's dying words to him were that she hoped Woodrow would remarry.

The mourning president took several vacations, accompanied by his daughter Margaret and Dr. Grayson, but nothing broke his depression—that is, until the day Wilson and Grayson were driving in a limousine through the streets of Washington. Grayson spotted Helen Bones, the president's cousin and the person who had been acting as White House hostess since the passing of the first lady. She was driving down the street in a car driven by a young woman, Edith Galt. In his book, *Dead Wake*, author Erik Larson described the woman as being "five feet nine inches tall, with a full and shapely figure and a taste for fine clothes . . . she was a striking woman, with a complexion and manner said to gleam, and eyes of a violet blue."

Galt was the widow of Norman Galt, the owner of a prestigious jewelry store in Washington. His death left her incredibly wealthy. She freely admitted that she had no interest in politics and couldn't name any of the candidates running for president.

When Wilson caught a glimpse of the young woman, he asked, "Who is that beautiful lady?" A few days later, Helen Bones invited her friend Edith to the White House for tea. When they arrived, they ran into the president as he was returning from a round of golf, and he decided to join the women. According to Bones, during the tea, she wasn't quite sure if she was imagining it or not, but Edith, with her cheerful disposition, made a comment that made the morose president suddenly laugh out loud. "[I wondered] if I was hearing right. I can't say that I foresaw in the first minute what was about to happen."

Edith Galt was invited back to the White House for dinner and took drives with the president and his cousin Helen on numerous occasions. By August 1914, Edith was a regular guest at the White House. Her light brought the president out of his depression, and one night, his spirits soaring with love, he asked Edith, sixteen years his junior, if she would marry him. Edith was surprised by the question and initially told him no, saying it was too soon after his wife had died for him to remarry. But over the next few months, the couple's love for each other grew. In a June 17, 1915, letter to Woodrow, Edith wrote:

I cannot let you go without just this little message to take the place of our goodnight talks and tell you again I love you . . . Thank you again for all the tender little things that make me feel your love.

In September, Wilson wrote to Edith:

You have the greatest soul, the noblest nature, the sweetest, most loving heart I have ever known, and my love, my reverence, my admiration for you, have increased in one evening as I should have thought only a lifetime of intimate, loving association could have increased them. You are more wonderful and lovely in my eyes than you ever were before.

Months later, after the subject of marriage had seemingly drifted from memory, Edith, Helen, a chauffeur, and the president were driving through a park in Washington, DC, when Edith unexpectedly put her arms around Wilson's neck and said, "Well, if you won't ask me, I will volunteer." She brought up the subject of marriage again, and that night, the couple became engaged. Despite concerns voiced by his cabinet about how his remarrying so soon after his previous wife's death would be perceived, they married on December 18, 1915.

President Wilson and Edith had grown extremely close even before their marriage. Despite her avowed disinterest in politics, she would indulge the president when he confided in her regarding issues of state, and after becoming First Lady, he would share important documents with her, including highly classified materials.

Edith was not your typical first lady. She was not partial to throwing White House socials and gatherings. Her prime interest in life was the health and comfort of her husband. But when the United States entered World War I on April 2, 1917, Edith became a role model—not only for women, but the entire country—as she led the way, showing Americans how to economize and help with the war effort. Edith and the president's daughters became Red Cross volunteers at a local canteen for soldiers. She wore clothes purchased at thrift stores. She began a wartime tradition of economizing by having Meatless Mondays and Wheatless Wednesdays at the White House. She knitted wool hats and blankets for soldiers, even organized war bond drives that featured Hollywood celebrities, including actors Charlie Chaplin and Douglas Fairbanks.

Edith's most famous contribution to the war effort was how she addressed the task of mowing the massive White House lawn. Instead of hiring gardeners to do the work, she borrowed twenty sheep from a nearby farm to graze on the lawn. In the fall, the wool would be sheared and sold at auction. One such auction netted over $52,000, all of which was donated to the American Red Cross.

Years before he began his term as president, Wilson had suffered a major health crisis. One morning in May 1906, he woke up with no sight in his left eye, pain in his left shoulder, and some paralysis in his right hand. A Philadelphia ophthalmologist, Dr. George de Schweinitz, examined Wilson and determined that he had suffered a transient ischemic attack (TIA), or mini stroke. Although he eventually recovered, his body was never the same. As Wilson's presidential inauguration drew near, physician and novelist Silas Weir Mitchell wrote that he could not see how the president-elect would ever be able to complete his first term in office.

In April 1919, as Wilson was negotiating a peace agreement with European leaders to end the Great War, he was stricken with a severe case of influenza. This drained his energy, already depleted by working around the clock to end the war. Slowly, he lost weight, became pale, and, to many observers, very frail. He began complaining about ferocious headaches, and the asthma attacks he was prone to became more uncontrollable. Still, it didn't stop Wilson from mounting a long whistle-stop tour of the United States in an attempt to gain public support for the treaty he had tentatively agreed to with European leaders, and the notion that the United States should join the League of Nations, a new organization whose goal would be to foster world peace.

Accompanying the president on his travels was his wife, as well as his personal physician, Dr. Grayson. On September 25, 1919, while at a stop in Pueblo, Colorado, Edith found her husband experiencing severe nausea. His facial muscles were twitching and he complained of a raging headache. Dr. Grayson examined Wilson and noted a "curious drag or looseness at the left side of his mouth." It appeared he had suffered another mini stroke. The tour was immediately canceled, and the presidential party returned to the White House.

There are two versions of what happened next on the morning of October 2, 1919. The one generally accepted is described in A. Scott Berg's biography, *Wilson*:

> *Edith had been having troubles of her own getting through the night, as she awakened frequently in order to monitor her husband's rest. At dawn on October 2, she found him sleeping soundly, but then around 8:30, he was sitting on the side of his bed reaching for a water bottle. As she handed it to him, she noticed his hand had gone limp. "I have no feeling in my hand," he said.*

Edith tried to support him and help him to the bathroom. As they walked, she couldn't help but notice that he had spasms of pain with each step he took. She asked her husband if she could leave him for a moment to call the doctor. He said yes. Instead of going to a phone near the bedroom, Edith went to a separate line and directly contacted Dr. Grayson. While on the phone, she heard a noise from the bedroom, and when she returned, she found the president lying on the floor, unconscious. He had suffered a massive stroke, leaving his left side paralyzed, his vision diminished, and his speech impaired.

There was no clear mechanism at this time for the transfer of power in the event that a president became gravely ill. The only rule was that he would either have to die or resign in order to relinquish his office to the vice president. Fearing for the president's reputation, and the office itself, Edith and Grayson attempted to cover up the severity of the president's condition. Edith would not allow any congressmen or senators—even members of his own cabinet—to speak with her husband. She only allowed Dr. Grayson and a few personal, trusted friends to meet with him. In the event the president did have to meet with someone, Edith would hide his paralyzed side with a blanket.

While the press knew Wilson was ill, they did not know the severity of the situation. Dr. Grayson kept the press notified of the president's condition, which he continually reported optimistically as being "good." In the meantime, Edith became the conduit between Wilson and the world. She would read through all of his reports and correspondence and determine which documents were significant enough to share with him. She would then report the president's decisions on specific matters to the appropriate cabinet members or members of the House and Senate.

In her memoir, Edith Wilson emphatically stated that she was only a steward for the president. "I, myself, never made a single decision regarding the disposition of public affairs. The only decision that was mine was what was important and what was not, and the very important decision of when to present matters to my husband." Still, the first lady did wield some power, as was the case when Secretary of State Robert Lansing called a cabinet meeting without notifying the president, and without him being in attendance. With Edith's urging, Lansing was removed from his position. Medical historian Jacob Appel wrote of Edith Wilson, "By deferring to the cabinet and tackling a number of high priority issues, Mrs. Wilson managed to keep the ship of state afloat."

What's even more remarkable about the events surrounding Woodrow Wilson's stroke and Edith Wilson's participation in the presidency is that these events were happening just as women were earning the right to vote.

Eventually, President Wilson was able to make more public appearances, although he never fully recovered. His second term in office ended in March 1921, and the couple retired to a house on S Street in Washington. Three years later, on February 3, 1924, the twenty-eighth president of the United States died. His last word was "Edith."

For the remainder of her life, Edith Wilson worked to keep her husband's legacy alive, asserting until her death that she had never been in control of the government. Even still, Edith Wilson was at the helm during a pivotal time in American history.

At the age of eighty-nine, Edith was invited to ride in the inaugural parade for president-elect John F. Kennedy in 1961. The *Washington Post* observed that "she continued to dress beautifully and was skilled enough with the needle to whip up a hat for herself when the fancy strikes."

Eleven months later, Edith Wilson passed away, leaving behind an incredible story of the "first" female US president.

FOOTNOTE TO HISTORY:
THERE HAD TO BE A FIRST

While the wife of President Woodrow Wilson was not technically the president of the United States after her husband's stroke, as we have seen, she could arguably be called the first female president, having taken on many of his responsibilities. Since that time, many women have tried but failed to be elected to the highest office in the land. Some were more famous than others, like Elizabeth Dole, wife of Senator Bob Dole, in 2000; Michelle Bachman in 2012; Hillary Rodham Clinton in 2016; and Kamala Harris in 2024. But the first woman to run for the office was in 1872. Her name was Victoria Claflin Woodhull.

Born into poverty in Ohio, Woodhull married the much older Dr. Canning Woodhull when she was fifteen years old, only to find he was an incurable drunkard. From that moment on, the young woman had to fend for herself, working many different jobs over the years until she and her sister Tennie became acquainted with railroad tycoon Cornelius Vanderbilt, who befriended the young women and provided them with stock market tips. Acting on those tips, the sisters eventually amassed a fortune, opening their own brokerage firm in 1870.

By becoming one of the first women to open a Wall Street brokerage, Woodhull was emboldened to fight for women's and workers' rights, as well as for the poor. After the Sixteenth Amendment—allowing women the right to vote—failed to pass Congress, she was invited to speak before the House Judiciary Committee, where she urged politicians to take another stab at passing the amendment. Although her efforts failed, she did gain the attention of suffrage leaders Susan B. Anthony and Elizabeth Cady Stanton, who encouraged her to make a run for the presidency on the Equal Rights Party ticket.

With famed abolitionist Frederick Douglass named as her running mate (he never did officially accept the nomination), Woodhull ran in the 1872 presidential election against the likes of Ulysses S. Grant and Horace Greeley. Her candidacy never gained much momentum, and it quickly ran into an obstacle. Woodhull was embroiled in a controversy with the American public after being the first in America to publish the works of communist Karl Marx, as well as an article that accused a well-known and well-respected Brooklyn, New York, clergyman, Henry Ward Beecher, of adultery with the wife of his friend, Theodore Tilton. And with that, her run for the presidency quietly ended. Nevertheless, Victoria Woodhull is recognized by historians as the first woman in America to run for president.

· 17 ·

MELTON BARKER,
THE KIDNAPPER'S FOIL,
AND ITINERANT FILMS

From the earliest days of motion pictures, average, everyday people have been fascinated with the medium and have dreamed of being in the pictures—sometimes with the goal of becoming a star, but usually just to see themselves on the silver screen. This continues today, with many people clamoring to be on one of a hundred different reality TV shows.

With this in mind, a new form of entrepreneurship appeared, not only in American cities and towns but internationally as well, in places like the United Kingdom, Australia, and New Zealand. It was a business model created by filmmakers that cashed in on this human desire. Some have called it a scam perpetrated by snake-oil salesmen on unsuspecting victims, but when we take a deeper look, it turns out that it was far from a racket. Call them what you will—con artists, scammers, salesmen—the truth is, these filmmakers didn't promise residents in countless towns across America that they would be in a movie and then flee town with their money in hand. For the most part, these filmmakers were true to their word, creating motion pictures by the hundreds, starring regular people from the many towns they traveled to. The general rule was that if a town had a population of at least 5,000, it would be a good place to film a movie and make a profit. The only thing these filmmakers never promised was that the "actors" would become stars.

This genre, called *itinerant films,* came on the scene in the early days of filmmaking, around 1914, long before sound was introduced, and continued well after talkies arrived, as late as the early 1970s. The idea was simple enough: These filmmakers believed the general public and local politicians would be willing to pay to see themselves and their neighbors on the big screen—and they were right.

The movies were made on a hit-and-run schedule, taking anywhere from a few days to a month to complete. The films were 100-foot two-reelers that were only valuable for a brief period of time in the town where they were filmed. Once the film had debuted in the local theater and run for a few days, it was either discarded or lost. Very few have survived, and today these glimpses into America's past reside in either private collections or have been digitalized and preserved in state archives, providing us with a historical record of a time—and in many cases, towns—that no longer exist.

There were dozens if not hundreds of itinerant filmmakers crisscrossing the country making these movies. They would travel from town to town, often with bloated résumés touting their Hollywood experience as talent scouts and public relations gurus. The films would be made with the most basic of film equipment, a small crew, and a promise to the town and its residents that they would be in the movies, but they would have to pay a small fee for the honor. (More on that in a moment.) The filmmakers would often obtain financial backing from the local chamber of commerce to help foot the bill for producing the movie, with the guarantee that they would be allowed to select locations around town that they wanted highlighted in the film.

Meanwhile, local theaters would also chip in by pledging that upon completion, the two-reeler films would do a short run at the theater. The short movies would run just before the main feature, and since most of the town wanted to see their friends, families, and neighbors on the big screen, the theater was virtually guaranteed a paying audience. Local businesses also had a hand in the production, often offering needed furnishings to add to a scene. In one movie filmed by itinerant film director Don O. Newland, called *Belvidere's Hero*, two local shops donated items to the production and were given their own title cards at the beginning of the movie: "Interior Decorations by Whitbeck & Johnson Furniture Company" and "Portraits by James Nott Studio."

In the end, the filmmakers would make just enough profit to allow them to move on to the next town and make the next movie. The movies were extremely limited in distribution, since they focused only on a specific community. While the film was popular in one town (where it was filmed), there would be no interest whatsoever in the neighboring town. As film historian Stephen Bottomore put it in an essay for the British Film Institute (BFI), these films would "put an audience to sleep fifteen to twenty miles away [from where it was shot]."

In an interview with KERA-TV in Dallas, Texas, Hugh V. Jamieson, who started producing his own itinerant films in 1913, said that he would arrive in town and take a room in a local hotel. After settling in, he would set up funding for the movie and begin casting. When filming was complete, he would develop the film in complete darkness in his hotel room's bathtub, then take the wet film and stretch it out across chairs, tables, and the bed so it could dry before editing it.

There were many itinerant filmmakers in the early 1900s, and each movie they made had its own unique script. While the scripts and plots (what plots there were) were different from producer to producer, they did have one thing in common: Each filmmaker had one script that they would produce over and over again. The only thing that would change would be the actors who starred in the film, for the most part, townspeople. Sometimes the filmmaker would change the title of the movie so it appeared as if it were unique to a particular town. For example, Don O. Newland and his company, Interstate Film Producers, cranked out a series of films between 1920 and 1930 called the "Hero" series. For each town he visited, Newland changed the title of the movie. If he visited Janesville, Wisconsin, the movie would be called *Janesville's Hero*; in Tyrone, Pennsylvania, *Tyrone's Hero*; and so forth.

As with all itinerant films, the plot was flimsy to say the least, with only slight variations made to accommodate a town's ambience and character. In the Hero series, the plot was: A boy falls in love with a local girl and wants to marry her, but her parents forbid it. The boy takes the girl on a "date," which is a tour of the town (how romantic for the girl, who already lives there), visiting the many industries and shops (cue the chamber of commerce travelogue). There is a fire at the girl's home, and the boy rescues the girl while the town's fire department fights the blaze. The parents now approve of the marriage, boy marries girl, the end. The one thing that separates the Hero series from other itinerant films is that it had some special effects tossed in. During the fire scene, the film turns from black-and-white to full red to symbolize the fire. The smoke from the building looks to be produced mechanically from behind a bush in front of the "burning" house.

Other notable itinerant filmmakers included Richard Norman, who reportedly filmed the movie *The Wrecker* more than forty times across the Midwest and Southeast, using this method of film production. Norman was known for more than just his itinerant films. He is famous for creating the Black (or "race") film genre, where an all-Black cast would star in the movie. These films actually had regional and national distribution and made a decent profit for his studio. The most famous of these was *The Flying Ace* (1926).

Of all the many itinerant movie producers, there is one whose personal biography is quite murky to historians even though his films are well quite well known to film buffs: Ennis Melton Barker, or simply Mel Barker. His Melton Barker Productions and Melton Barker Juvenile Productions produced a series of films starring "The Local Gang," a blatant reworking of the *Our Gang* or *Little Rascals* shorts.

Barker was born in Mississippi in 1903 and grew up in various towns across Texas. He was married three times during his life, with his first marriage taking place in 1926. Throughout his life and career, Barker claimed he was a successful filmmaker from Hollywood, making the claim that he had discovered Spanky McFarland from the Hal Roach *Our Gang* and *Little Rascal* series, which may have some merit. Whether or not his Spanky claim is true, he took the concept of the *Our Gang* shorts and ran with it. Beginning in 1930, Barker and his film companies began creating a series of films titled *The Kidnapper's Foil*, featuring "The Local Gang."

The Local Gang consisted of—you guessed it—local kids from whatever town he was in. Barker would recruit the local newspaper to run a story to attract potential actors:

> *Casting Director Arrives to Give "Kiddies" Movie Tests: Entries are pouring in to the office of the [insert theater name here] for the two-reel, all-talking kid movie to be made here soon, using local children from 3 to 12 years of age.*

The article went on to describe the application process. After submitting the application form that appeared at the end of the article, asking for the applicant's basic information—name, age, phone number, and if they were a boy or girl—the applicant would be informed when and where to arrive for an audition. In the end, Barker would use 100 to 125 children in the production, with a handful being selected to play main characters. The parents of these children were required to pay a small fee, usually $10, for their child to be in the film. Considering his first films were made during the Great Depression, this was an exorbitant amount of money for families to fork over. The fee included two to three days of training on how to act in front of a camera before filming would begin.

As with all itinerant films, the *Kidnapper's Foil* series follows the same plot over and over. A girl named Bette Davis (no relation to the famous actress) is kidnapped by two men who demand a ransom for her safe return. Drama ensues as a multitude of children from town set out to search for the girl. In the end, Bette is rescued, the kidnapping plot is thwarted, and the gang collects the reward money, which they use, just like in any good *Our Gang* comedy, to "put on a show," although in the *Kidnapper's Foil* series, they are called parties.

The acting is, to put it gently, interesting, with stilted lines read directly into the camera. The edits are *very* quick, jumping from a shot of one of the gang reading a line to the camera to the next as the rest of the gang sits on the ground, staring mesmerized into the camera. The party scene showcases several local children performing—some tap-dancing, some crooning a song, others performing acrobatic tricks. After each act, there is another quick cut to all of the kids sitting or standing around together, applauding. The applause is abruptly cut, and it's on to the next performance. Several scenes are simple group shots of the 100-plus group of kids fast-walking or running toward the camera.

In a 2005 interview with the *Austin American-Statesman*, Caroline Frick, a film historian whose mission it has been to trace Melton Barker's history, was asked to give her opinion of the movies. "They're so bad, they're good." When asked to comment on whether Barker had any real filmmaking abilities, Frick said, "Let's put it this way: In cinematic talent? No. In corralling children? Very impressive."

Once the movie had been developed and edited, another article would appear in the local newspaper, this time with headlines that really grabbed the reader: "Little [town name] Girl Is Kidnapped; Released When Hideout Found." Now that they had your attention, the article went on to describe the movie and when it would play at the local theater.

Melton Barker died in 1977, and today, film students and historians look at his and other itinerant movies for what they were: a glimpse into our past, and an incredibly unique business model where both the filmmaker and theater profited, the chamber of commerce had a chance to highlight important sites and industry around town, and thousands of children along with their families and friends got to see themselves on the big screen. The odds against any of these kids becoming movie stars in Hollywood were astronomical, but at least they could say they had had a role in a movie.

When asked about those who suggested these moviemakers were modern-day snake oil salesmen, Melton Barker said those people were ignorant, and he had grown tired of them lambasting his work. "The kids get a big kick out of being in a movie," he said, "and besides, I work too hard for this to be a fake."

FOOTNOTE TO HISTORY: THE FIRST KISS CONTROVERSY

The film only lasted a total of eighteen minutes, and the kiss portrayed in the film, only two seconds, but what Thomas Edison had brought to the fledgling film industry in 1896 would titillate and shock audiences around the world.

The motion picture industry was in its infancy in 1895, and the films were quite different from the three-plus-hour blockbusters we see today. American inventor Thomas Edison and the Lumière Brothers of Lyon, France, were the pioneers of this new "dream factory," creating short films of common, everyday people doing common, everyday things. They created short, twenty-second films of boxing matches, workers leaving a factory after a shift, even a person sneezing. One of the most startling films produced at this time had women shrieking in fear, men hiding their faces in horror, and children sitting on the edge of their seats with excitement: a film of a huge steam locomotive heading straight toward the audience from the screen.

Edison filmed his early short movies in a tar-paper-clad shack at his lab in Menlo Park, New Jersey, dubbed the Black Maria. One side of the building's roof could be opened to let sunshine in for proper lighting. The building itself sat on a circular track that allowed it to be rotated so it always had optimal sunlight. It was here in 1895 that Edison filmed one of his most memorable shorts, and the most shocking of the time, called *The Kiss.*

Edison and director William Heise recruited actors May Irwin and John Rice to re-create the memorable kiss scene from their hit stage comedy, *The Widow Jones.* By today's standards, the kiss that was filmed is mute and laughable. The couple is seen sitting together in an awkward pose, their cheeks firmly pressed together. Rice sits up, fiddles with his bristling mustache, much like Snidely Whiplash would do in future episodes of *The Rocky and Bullwinkle Show,* then kisses Irwin. The end.

When it was released, Edison's movie company advertised the film by saying, "They get ready to kiss, begin to kiss, and kiss and kiss and kiss in a way that brings the house down every time." And it certainly did. Critics either loved the short or hated it. The *New York World* newspaper bubbled with excitement over the film, writing, "For the first time in the history of the world it is possible to see what a kiss looks like . . . The real kiss is a revelation."

Some critics were not so generous. One reviewer wrote, "The spectacle of the prolonged pasturing on each other's lips was beastly enough in life size on the stage but magnified to gargantuan proportions and repeated three times over is absolutely disgusting." The film was deemed to be pornographic. At the Vatican, the Pope denounced it and called for immediate censorship of such filth, labeled "a threat to public morality."

As with all such episodes, the ruckus caused by *The Kiss* quickly dissipated. Things would quickly become more risqué as the world of celluloid began to test the boundaries of how far they could go when it came to morality in pictures. Later the same year as *The Kiss* was released, *Le Coucher de la Mariée* ("Bedtime for the Bride," or "The Bridegroom's Dilemma") was released in France, a seven-minute silent film about a bride and groom getting ready to consummate their marriage. The woman is taking off her clothes for the entirety of the film, stopping at her unmentionables just as the movie ends. Blasphemy.

The door was now open for more and more daring and risqué films. If the Pope thought *The Kiss* was obscene, he surely wasn't ready for the types of films the motion picture industry would make in the decades to come.

· 18 ·

THE BATTLE OF LOS ANGELES

Today, in the twenty-first century, we are always within arm's reach of our cell phones, the device's cheerfully pinging tones alerting us to incoming messages, severe weather alerts, and more throughout the day. But an alert of an incoming nuclear missile attack? That's what happened on January 13, 2018, when cell phones across Hawaii went off, displaying the message, "Ballistic missile threat inbound Hawaii. Seek immediate shelter. This is not a drill." Electronic signs along highways shouted the same dire warning.

North Korean dictator Kim Jong-un had been making threatening overtures against the United States for months by lobbing test missiles from launchers on the Korean peninsula into the Pacific Ocean. Each launch of the rockets proved the country's potential for rocketing nuclear warheads closer and closer to the Hawaiian Islands chain. Needless to say, residents and tourists were jittery about the real possibility of nuclear annihilation and took immediate action.

As emergency sirens wailed, thousands of people began running for shelter. Highways were jammed with people running in terror, wondering what to do. State representative Matt LoPresti told CNN that he gathered his family and headed to an interior bathroom where they got into the bathtub and began to pray. One woman told reporters that she truly felt she was going to die. "I drove to get my kids even though I knew I probably wouldn't make it. I was visualizing what was happening while I was on the road. It was awful."

The alert lasted thirty-eight minutes, and then a second alert was sent out, giving the "all clear." Several officials on the island said it was just a test of the island's alert system. As it turns out, it was human error. During a shift change at the island's emergency command post, somebody flipped the wrong switch, resulting in panic and terror sweeping across the islands.

It is easy to see that given the right set of circumstances—a tense international political climate for starters—an alert such as this could easily put people on edge, anticipating disaster that may, or may not, occur at any moment. A comparable situation happened decades before in Los Angeles in February of 1942, but that alert was sparked by an actual military attack 2,500 miles to the west.

While no one saw the event coming, it should have been anticipated. As the sun rose over the beautiful Hawaiian island of Oahu on a Sunday morning in December 1942, some families were preparing to go to church, while others were planning a day at the beach. Many of the enlisted men stationed at the small naval base of Pearl Harbor were sleeping in after dancing the night away at one of the island's clubs. It was a peaceful tropical scene if ever there was one—that is, until 7:55 a.m. when a Japanese plane flew overhead. The brilliant red circle, symbol of the Imperial Rising Sun, glared down menacingly over the ships at anchor in the harbor as the first bomb dropped. In just over one hour, much of the American fleet stationed on the island was destroyed; 2,335 servicemen and 68 civilians were killed, with an additional 1,178 wounded. World War II, which was already waging in the far western Pacific Ocean and across Europe, had come to America.

Following the Japanese attack on Pearl Harbor, cities, towns, and villages up and down the West Coast of the United States feared they would be next, especially the city of Los Angeles. With a population of over 1.5 million in 1942, Los Angeles and its surrounding suburbs was home to some of the largest and most productive aircraft manufacturing companies in the world. In San Pedro Bay, companies like Craig Shipbuilding were busy churning out commercial and naval vessels. San Pedro was also the home of the San Pedro Naval Base, where sixteen battleships, fourteen cruisers, and 31,286 navy personnel were billeted. If the Japanese were to strike the US mainland, the target would most likely be Los Angeles, and residents were on edge.

To add fuel to the already increasing angst of the city's residents, Los Angeles was also home to over 23,000 Japanese Americans, a figure that left LA residents wondering whether they could be trusted. The LA Police Department had begun accusing Japanese citizens of signaling enemy aircraft, though no evidence of this actually happening was ever presented.

Those fears of an imminent Japanese attack along the West Coast only intensified when on December 23, 1941, only sixteen days after the bombing of Pearl Harbor, a Japanese submarine sank the oil tanker SS *Montebello* and the merchant ship SS *Absaroka* off the California coast, killing one seaman. The Japanese were mounting a campaign against the US mainland directly, if not with physical destruction, then with psychological warfare. They were proving that the United States was not immune to war.

On February 23, 1942, at 7:58 p.m., a yellow alert was sent out by naval intelligence due to suspected Japanese activity in the waters off the coast of Southern California. The alert warned local civil defense and residents that an attack could be expected within the next ten hours. Local radio stations were shut down, and a blackout went into effect. They were correct in their assumption. The Japanese submarine *I-17* was lurking off the coast, 70 miles northwest of Los Angeles, near the Ellwood Oil Field in Santa Barbara County. Minutes after the alert went out, residents who lived near the oil field were startled when several explosions were heard.

Ten-year-old J. J. Hollister III was listening to President Roosevelt's Fireside Chat on the radio with his family when the shooting began. "In a moment or two," Hollister recalled, "we heard a whistling noise and a thump as a projectile hit near the house." The family rushed outside to see flashes in the night near the oil field.

The submarine had surfaced, and using its 5.5-inch deck guns, had begun shooting at the oil field before submerging and hightailing it out of the area. It was the first direct attack on the US mainland of the war. No one was injured, but the shooting did damage a pump house and one oil derrick. It was reported that some of the shooting nearly took out an aviation fuel tank, which would have been catastrophic. While the attack inflicted only minor damage on the refinery, it did accomplish its main objective—a psychological victory—leaving the residents of Santa Barbara, Ventura, and Los Angeles counties frightened and on edge, fearing the worst was yet to come. The all clear was finally sounded at 10:23 p.m.

In the early-morning hours of February 25, a radar site reported that an aerial contact approximately 120 miles off the coast of Los Angeles was rapidly approaching the city. An alert went out for antiaircraft batteries to prepare for battle. The US Army Air Forces was also alerted but decided to keep their aircraft on the ground, taking a wait-and-see posture.

The radar site continued to monitor the incoming object until it disappeared, but even still, at 2:21 a.m., the regional defense coordinator ordered a region-wide blackout. Air-raid sirens began to blare, and pandemonium ensued. Antiaircraft guns and searchlights began scanning the skies. Suddenly, switchboards at police stations were deluged with phone calls. Twenty-five planes were reported over LA, then balloons carrying red flares—bombs?—were reported. Swarms of additional planes ranging in number from 1 to 700 were "spotted." "I could barely see the planes," artilleryman Charles Patrick was quoted as saying, "but they were there all right."

Historians with the Museum of the City of San Francisco aptly describe what happened next: "[At this point,] the air over Los Angeles erupted like a volcano." The Battle of Los Angeles had begun. Three-inch antiaircraft guns came to life with a dazzling array of shells bursting in the night sky and the sound of machine-gun fire echoed down the streets. Many people on the ground were injured and several killed as a result of the melee. The *Los Angeles Times* reported three people were killed in car accidents along the blacked-out streets; two more died from heart attacks. Many injuries occurred, including a radio announcer who ran into an awning in the darkness that severely gashed his forehead. A police officer who was attempting to break into a business that had left their lights on during the blackout ended up with a horribly gashed leg from kicking in the store's front window to gain access.

Air-raid wardens suffered the highest number of injuries, as they, like police officers, attempted to break into buildings to put out lights. One fell as he scaled a wall to an apartment and broke his leg; another sprained an ankle jumping a 3-foot fence; still another broke his arm tumbling down his own front steps in the darkness. The antiaircraft fire caused the most damage, with shrapnel from the exploding shells raining down on the city, blowing out car tires, damaging roofs of cars, even demolishing portions of homes and garages.

For over an hour, the barrage continued as terrified citizens scrambled for shelter. Over 1,400 rounds of antiaircraft shells were fired. As dawn approached, the all clear was finally given, but military officials, civil defense authorities, and residents alike were confused. As the sun rose, they realized that no Japanese aircraft had flown over the city. No bombs were dropped, no enemy paratroopers landed.

Once the smoke had cleared, the controversy began. Secretary of War Henry Stimpson took the US Army's position that at least fifteen Japanese planes had actually flown over the city and the air raid was warranted. Secretary of the Navy Frank Knox released a statement saying that the raid was a false alarm. Distrust over the conflicting accounts raged. An editorial in the *New York Times* three days later said:

> *If the batteries were firing on nothing at all, as Secretary Knox implies, it is a sign of expensive incompetence and jitters. If the batteries were firing on real planes, some of them as low as 9,000 feet, as Secretary Stimson declares, why were they completely ineffective? Why did no American plane go up to engage them, or even to identify them? . . . What would have happened if this had been a real air raid? . . . An immediate investigation, a clear statement to the public, and a prompt rectification of the conditions which made this incident possible are imperative.*

The *Washington Post* called the Battle of Los Angeles a "recipe for jitters." Some congressmen declared that it was all a scheme to scare the 1.5 million residents and force the war industry in the region to move elsewhere. Still others believed it was alien flying saucers spotted over the city that had caused the panic.

In the end, the Battle of Los Angeles was attributed to a series of weather balloons that had been released earlier in the week. Military officials deemed the air raid "a success," stating that it was an excellent example of how the nation's coastal defenses were up to the challenge of protecting the country. The mayor of Los Angeles at the time, Fletcher Bowron, told a *New York Times* reporter that his city "was glad to be a guinea pig if this was a practice maneuver."

The fear the Japanese had instilled in Americans living on the West Coast that an attack was imminent had grave consequences that rippled across the region. Six days before the "attack," President Franklin Delano Roosevelt had issued Executive Order 9066. The controversial order directed the government to round up and incarcerate Japanese Americans. By the night of the LA air raid, weeks before the executive order was signed and put into effect, the LA Police Department had already jailed twenty Japanese Americans who they believed were agents of the Imperial government.

On February 14, just over two weeks prior to the air raid, the US Navy announced that all persons of Japanese ancestry were to leave Terminal Island near the San Pedro naval base. By February 27, the FBI had already begun arresting and removing Japanese family heads from the region. On March 2, Public Proclamation Number 1 was issued, dividing the West Coast into two primary military zones, with Area #1 being subdivided into a "prohibited zone" due to its military bases and factories, and where persons of Japanese, German, or Italian ancestries would need to evacuate. Over 9,000 who met the qualifications moved to Area #2 voluntarily, but eventually, many of those people would be forcibly evacuated out of the region altogether. Over the next six months, more than 122,000 men, women, and children were forcibly relocated to internment camps.

While the Battle of Los Angeles is now a faded memory, it has gained some attention over the years. On the lighter side, a comedy titled *1941*, directed by Stephen Spielberg and starring *Saturday Night Live* alums Dan Aykroyd and John Belushi, was released in 1979. Although the title was off by a year, the movie is a fictional comedy based on the events of the LA air raid.

On a more serious note, the air raid is memorialized annually during the annual reenactment at the Fort MacArthur Museum in Los Angeles. The fort was opened in 1914 and became a museum in 1985, housing fascinating artifacts curated from the defenses that protected the US West Coast during World War II and the Battle of Los Angeles.

FOOTNOTE TO HISTORY: A FUTILE BOMBARDMENT

The attack on the Ellwood Oil Field by the Japanese at the beginning of World War II came as quite a shock to Americans living along the US West Coast. While the attack wasn't on the US mainland, the Japanese would eventually launch others on the continental United States, with varying degrees of success.

One attack involved a series of balloons that were launched throughout 1944. The plan was for the Japanese military to construct these 33-foot-in-diameter balloons out of mulberry paper and fill them with hydrogen. Thirty-three-pound fragmentation bombs would be attached to each balloon. With an ingenious use of timers and timed fuses, the military would launch the balloons, also known as *fu-go* bombs, from Japan into the jet stream, where they would float 5,000 miles across the Pacific Ocean to the US mainland. The hope was that the bombs would explode over the dense northwestern forests and start massive wildfires that would divert American resources away from the war to fight the fires.

The first group of 9,000 balloons was launched on November 3, 1944, landing just off the California coast near San Pedro two days later. By November 6, balloons were landing in the Aleutian Islands, Canada, and as far east as Wyoming. Most of the bombs crashed without incident. One balloon, however, landed in Oregon, but did not explode. A minister's wife along with five Sunday school children exploring the woods found the bomb attached to the deflated balloon. All were killed as they attempted to drag the bomb back to their camp and it exploded.

The *fu-go* bombs were not the first time that the US mainland was attacked by the Japanese military. That came on June 21, 1942, when the submarine *I-25* launched an attack on Fort Stevens, a US military base located in Hammond, Oregon. Constructed in 1863 following the War of 1812, the fort was meant to guard the region against British ships that might try to venture up the Columbia River. By World War II, the fort had transformed from an earthen-and-wood structure to a massive concrete edifice that had the same mission: to protect the northwestern coast of the United States from enemy invasion.

In 1942, the US Navy had laid mines around the entrance to the Columbia River to prevent enemy vessels from approaching. On that June day, the *I-25* was waiting for local fishing vessels to return home to port. Staying submerged, the submarine's captain skillfully followed the returning boats into the harbor, thus avoiding all of the mines.

Around midnight, the sub surfaced near Fort Stevens and opened fire with its 140-millimeter deck guns. The problem was that it was midnight and the entire region was under blackout orders, so the guns were firing blindly at the shore. The fort's commander, Colonel Carl S. Donley, told his men to hold their fire, fearing that the flash from any gunfire would give away the fort's exact position, which was virtually invisible at that hour with its dark black paint color.

The commander was right; the attack was unsuccessful, with a nearby baseball field receiving the brunt of the damage. The headline in an article for the *New York Times* by reporter Lawrence E. Davies led the June 23 front page with the headline, "A Futile Bombardment on the Coast of Oregon."

As a result of the attack, and the "Battle of Los Angeles" that had occurred only months before, a full-fledged "Rehearsal for Disaster" was planned by civil defense authorities. This simulation of an actual bombing—involving 3,000 air-raid wardens, 1,000 auxiliary policemen, and 2,500 auxiliary firemen—would enable volunteers to become better organized and more vigilant in the event that the enemy surfaced off the coast again.

· 19 ·

HOW THE "CAPRICIOUS AND CANTANKEROUS" LIMPING LADY HELPED WIN WORLD WAR II

"The 'Donna Juanita' [a libretto about the female version of Don Juan] of the class now approaches," the 1924 Roland Park Country School for Girls yearbook entry began. "Though professing to hold man in contempt, Dindy is yet his closest counterpart—in costume. She is, by her own confession, cantankerous and capricious, but in spite of it all we would not do without her . . . She has been acclaimed the most original of our class, and she lives up to her reputation at all times. The one thing to expect from Dind is the unexpected."

Even during her formative years at the preparatory school in Baltimore, Maryland, Virginia Hall (better known to her friends and family as "Dindy") had a reputation of being extraordinary, excelling at everything she put her mind to—sports, writing, even acting in theater. She loved the outdoors, and more often than not you would find her hiking, horseback riding, or hunting. The latter would create an almost insurmountable obstacle to Hall's future career. During a hunting trip, she was climbing over a fence and her gun discharged, mangling her leg. She was fitted with a wooden prosthesis and had to relearn how to walk. The wooden leg, which she named "Cuthbert," gave her a decisive limp.

Virginia knew what she wanted, and the leg injury would not stop her from seeking a meaningful and fulfilling life, one that would offer adventure and make a difference in the world. Not content to be a homemaker or a clerical worker, Hall challenged the notion that women were not men's equal, and her accomplishments would prove that one hundred times over. In the end, Virginia Hall had the adventure she longed for and played a key role in helping the Allies beat the Nazis in World War II. Her adventures read like an Ian Fleming James Bond novel, only this story was real life.

Virginia Hall was born in 1906 to Barbara and Edwin Hall, destined to live a privileged, upper-class life in Baltimore, Maryland. Described as a bright and ambitious girl, Hall saw herself as equal to any man during a time when women had only just recently attained the right to vote, still mostly relegated to being homemakers. Hall attended Radcliffe and Barnard Colleges (part of Columbia University) and George Washington University. During her college life, Hall excelled in linguistics, including French, German, and Italian, as well as economics. She continued her studies in France, Germany, and Austria, with one goal in mind: to become a member of the US diplomatic corps.

While in Europe, Hall found work as a consular clerk—basically a secretarial job—with the US State Department in Venice and Tallinn (Estonia), an unsatisfying job for the adventurous young woman. She applied several times to become a diplomat with the US Foreign Service but was denied at each step because she was a woman. An application for employment as a diplomat with the US State Department in 1937 was declined due to her disability. Secretary of State Cordell Hull responded to Hall's application, writing, "Hall could become a fine career girl in the Consular Service." She appealed the decision to President Franklin D. Roosevelt, but was once again denied. In 1939, she resigned from the State Department.

Meanwhile, Europeans were closely watching the actions of Adolf Hitler and the Nazi Party in Germany. Hitler first expanded Germany's borders into Rhineland in 1936. In March 1938, he went on to annex Austria. In September 1938, in a move he believed would "appease" the German aggressor, British prime minister Neville Chamberlain agreed to allow Germany to take over a portion of Czechoslovakia known as Sudetenland. In September 1939, despite promising not to occupy any more territory in Europe, Hitler's army invaded Poland. World War II had begun.

By now, Virginia Hall was well acquainted with the nuances of life in various European towns and villages, especially in France, where she had a deep love for the people. With France declaring war on Germany, she wanted to do her part for the war effort, so she enlisted with the Organisation du Service Sanitaire de l'Armée, the French ambulance corps. She received first-aid training and soon began evacuating wounded soldiers and civilians from battlefields almost around the clock.

Upon the surrender of France to the German army in 1940, Hall fled to England, where she was offered a job at the US embassy, but once again as a clerk. After surviving the incessant bombing of London during the Blitz, Hall became even more determined to do her part in the war effort. On February 26, 1941, she once again resigned her position, this time for a much more important job. She became a special agent for the British Special Operations Executive (SOE)—a spy.

Known as "Churchill's Secret Army" or the "Baker Street Irregulars," the mission of the SOE was to gather intelligence for the British, conduct espionage, and routinely sabotage German supply line outposts, or, as the agency put it, "set Europe ablaze."

To say the work of the SOE was dangerous is an understatement. Out of 13,000 agents, 25 percent of them were women. Ultimately, 40 percent of the female agents were either executed by the Nazis or died in concentration camps.

After completing the SOE's elite instruction program that consisted of hand-to-hand combat, weapons, radio operation, demolition, and parachute training, Hall assumed the identity of Brigitte LeContre, an American reporter for the *New York Post*. Perfecting disguises was one of Hall's unique talents. According to author Sonia Purnell, Hall "could be four different women in the space of an afternoon, with four different code names."

Under the code name Germaine, Hall arrived in Lyon, France, on August 23, 1941, to begin her fifteen-month-long mission. During that time, Hall created the Heckler Network, a group of ordinary local people whom she could trust and rely upon to conduct missions, people who could avoid being detected by the Germans. Hall recruited everyone she could, from prostitutes to nuns.

Over the next fifteen months, Hall and her network rescued downed Allied airmen and returned them safely to Britain; organized, funded, and supplied the French Resistance; supervised Allied air drops that aided the Resistance; gathered intelligence on German troop movements; and organized sabotage efforts against German supply lines. Hall also organized and executed plans to extract prisoners of war from Nazi POW camps.

The defeats that Virginia Hall—dubbed "The Limping Lady"— laid upon the Germans were so devastating that she was declared the most "dangerous of all Allied spies" by the Germans. The head of Hitler's Gestapo, Klaus Barbie, was reported to have said "I would give anything to get my hands on that limping bitch." Virginia Hall was now topping the Nazis' most-wanted list. Posters with her image and the words "The Enemies' Most Dangerous Spy— We Must Find and Destroy Her" were circulated across France. The pressure was on, with the Germans in hot pursuit.

After Germany's defeat in North Africa in November 1942, Hitler moved his troops north into France, effectively flooding the region with soldiers. Hall knew that her escape routes would soon be cut off, and with only hours to spare before the Germans descended, she was driven south to a foot trail in the Pyrenees Mountains that would lead her into the neutral country of Spain. Her last message to London before embarking on the trail read, "Cuthbert is tiresome, but I can cope." The officer on duty, unfamiliar with her prosthetic leg's nickname, replied, "Have him eliminated."

The trail was a 44-mile hike across the summits of the 7,500-foot-tall mountains. It was mid-November, and Hall would face blinding snow and ice storms and ferocious frigid winds, all while climbing with Cuthbert. Hall's strength, determination, and endurance in escaping capture cannot be underestimated. The pain must have been excruciating. The amount of time it took her to make the frozen march is unknown, but eventually she arrived in Spain, where she was detained for twenty days due to crossing the border illegally without proper documentation. The US embassy in Spain was able to gain her release, and she made her way back to England.

Upon her return, Hall was awarded the British MBE (Member of British Empire), but declined accepting it, fearing it would blow her cover. Instead, she pressed the SOE to return her to France to continue her mission, but since she was now wanted by Hitler, they decided her talents would best be used on the home front, a dismal prospect for the spy. Undaunted, and with the begrudging approval of the SOE, Virginia Hall joined the US Office of Strategic Services (OSS), the forerunner of today's CIA. In May 1944, Hall donned another disguise, as an old woman. Her teeth were ground down, her hair was dyed gray, and she dressed the part. Her limp was disguised by acting as a shuffling old lady. Her theater training in prep school was coming in handy.

Under her new code name of Diane, Hall and a colleague arrived under the cloak of darkness off the coast of Brittany, France.

Quickly, she set up shop just south of Paris in the village of Maidou, where the pair would monitor and report on troop movements. Around May of 1944, Hall received new orders: She would be organizing and preparing the French Resistance in preparation for the invasion of Normandy by the Allies: D-Day. Having extensive experience already, Hall quickly contacted her old Resistance network and arranged for air drops by the Allies of supplies, weapons, and additional manpower.

As the fateful day of June 6, 1944, approached, all was ready and the Resistance workers were on the move, sabotaging German supply lines and disrupting troop movements by attacking them relentlessly. By August 26, 1944, Hall's Resistance fighters had proven to be such a formidable foe that the German southern command in Le Chambon surrendered to them.

On September 25, Hall and her team were pulled from the battlefield because it appeared the war was over. Returning to the United States, Hall was honored for her service and awarded the Distinguished Service Cross. In a letter to President Harry Truman, the head of the OSS, General William J. Donovan, wrote of Virginia Hall's extraordinary service:

> *Miss Virginia Hall, an American civilian working for this agency in the European Theatre of Operations, has been awarded the Distinguished Service Cross for extraordinary heroism in connection with military operations against the enemy. We understand that Miss Hall is the first civilian woman in this war to receive the DSC. Despite the fact that she was well known to the Gestapo, Miss Hall voluntarily returned to France in March 1944 to assist in sabotage operations against the Germans.*

Truman had requested that he be the one to present the award to Hall, publicly and in person, to honor her service and bravery, but Donovan insisted that her cover be protected. Instead,

Donovan presented the award himself in a private ceremony that was attended only by the general, Hall, and her mother. When presented the award, Hall made one comment: "Not bad for a girl from Baltimore." It was the only Distinguished Service Cross awarded to a civilian woman in World War II.

When the OSS was dismantled following the war, Hall applied yet again for a position with the US Foreign Service, but once again, was declined, this time due to postwar budget cuts. She did, however, obtain a field position in Europe with the Central Intelligence Group (later named the CIA) in 1947. She moved to New York to work with the CIA's National Committee for Free Europe, where she lived with a French American named Paul Goillot. They had met when he parachuted into France during one of the air drops, and they were married in 1950.

Virginia Hall continued her work in various capacities with the CIA until she reached the mandatory retirement age of sixty, after which she lived a quiet life with her husband on a farm in Barnesville, Maryland, where she enjoyed reading, bird watching, and playing with her pet poodles—quite a change after the adventures she had been on.

Virginia Hall died at the age of seventy-six on July 12, 1982. Her husband, Paul, passed away five years later. The incredible and heroic life story of Virginia Hall was hidden in the archives of the CIA for many years, but after her death, tales of her exploits began emerging. In 1988, the French government held a ceremony to open their new Military Intelligence Hall of Fame. During the ceremony, Hall was posthumously awarded the government's Croix de Guerre avec Palme, presented to those who fought with the Allies during the war. And in 2006, she was honored once again by French and British ambassadors in a ceremony at the French ambassador's home in Washington, DC.

Not bad for a girl from Baltimore, indeed.

FOOTNOTE TO HISTORY:
LEAVE IT TO "Q" DIVISION

"[It's] an explosive alarm clock, guaranteed to never wake anyone who uses it."

Such was the dry sense of humor of the character simply known as "Q" in the James Bond movies. The abbreviation is short for "quartermaster." What is less certain is whether the moniker was for a single person or a department of the British spy agency, MI6. It is generally recognized as the man himself, played by actor Desmond Llewelyn in seventeen Bond films. With each movie, the gadgets he provided for Bond became increasingly more sophisticated, and outlandish: a cigarette laced with cyanide; a rocket-firing cigarette; a ski-pole gun; explosive eyeglasses. The list is endless.

While Bond's gadgets make for thrilling spy adventures on the big screen, there were actually men and women who designed and implemented clever tools such as these to aid the nation's spies in defeating our adversaries. Spycraft became extremely important during World War II, for both the Allies and the Axis. One of the many US teams developing clandestine devices was led by Captain Robley E. Winfrey, who was based at Fort Hunt in Virginia, code-named "P.O. Box 1142." Winfrey and his team, as well as other spymasters from around the world, devised ingenious implements to spy on the enemy, devices that even Q would be proud of, many of which are on display at the Spyscape Spy Museum and Experience in New York City:

- ■ Radio suitcase: Used by British intelligence, this high-powered radio fit neatly into an ordinary suitcase and could be operated by battery, or by the energy created from pedaling a bicycle.

- ■ Glove gun: A pair of hand gloves with a concealed single-shot pistol inside.

- ■ Kiss of death lipstick: The container for this French lipstick had a secret compartment that contained deadly cyanide pills.

- ■ Pencil dagger: It looks and writes like an ordinary number-two pencil, but pull on both ends and a deadly dagger is revealed.

- ■ Invisible ink matches: Don't light them up; write with them. These matches had a special coating that could write messages invisibly.

- ■ Exploding rats: Literally hundreds of rats were procured by the US SOE (Special Operations Executive) office during World War II. The rats—dead, of course—were skinned, dissected, filled with explosives, then stitched back up. The rats were to have been placed strategically throughout German military posts next to boilers in coal bins. The idea was that once spotted, the Germans would toss the dead rodent into the boiler and poof! The building would blow up. The plan never came off, however, because the Germans discovered the plot and intercepted the rats.

· 20 ·

A FEMME FATALE, A POISON PEN, AND A KILLER MILKSHAKE

The first paragraph in a March 10, 1975, *Washington Post* article set the scene: "Press accounts have identified Cuba's Fidel Castro as the target of an unsuccessful CIA assassination plot. The headlines couldn't have come at a worse time for Secretary of State Henry A. Kissinger, who was in the thick of 'most delicate' negotiations, according to White House sources, to restore some kind of diplomatic relationship with Cuba."

This wasn't the first time that an assassination plot by the United States against the Cuban leader was reported in the *Washington Post*. In fact, since the dictator had begun his reign over the Caribbean nation, there had been six other attempts, some ingenious, others almost slapstick, reminiscent of an old Keystone Cops silent movie. Throughout his life, Castro was a thorn in the side of the United States, and in particular, the CIA. In their eyes, he had to be dealt with one way or another.

Castro began his climb to the top as dictator of the Caribbean island in 1953, when he led a group of 160 rebels in an attack on the second-largest military base on the island, Moncada Barracks, in what he believed would be the start of his revolution to oust then Cuban president, Fulgencio Batista. The heavily defended base was no match for Castro's rebels, and they were easily turned back, with over half of his men captured or killed. Castro himself was captured and sentenced to fifteen years in prison for the coup attempt, but two years later, Batista granted amnesty to all political prisoners, and Castro was released. Soon after, Castro and a group of eighty-one men attempted another coup, and again, most of his men were killed. After this second failed attempt, other revolutionary groups banded together with Castro, and in 1958, after the United States cut all aid to the Batista government, Cuban rebels were able to topple the Batista regime and Castro was sworn in as the Cuban prime minister.

Initially, the United States recognized the Castro government as legitimate, but after nationalizing American assets on the island and declaring a Marxist government, the United States felt they needed to act, to rid the Western world of this perceived threat to its security. With aid and training by the CIA, Cuban exiles who had fled to the United States were recruited to invade the island with the goal of uprooting the Castro regime in what was known as the Bay of Pigs Invasion. Harsh weather, soggy equipment, and lack of ammunition caused the invasion to fail miserably. The Soviet Union reacted to the attack by increasing their presence and influence over the island. They began shipping nuclear-armed ballistic missiles to Cuba—a move that would push the two great superpowers, and the world, to the brink of nuclear war, in what became known as the Cuban Missile Crisis.

Beginning only months after Castro's overthrow of Batista and just prior to the Bay of Pigs Invasion, the first CIA assassination attempts began, many involving shady dealings with organized crime figures. One of the first included the recruitment of gangster John "Handsome Johnny" Roselli. Roselli rose to prominence in the mob world when he became an associate of Al Capone, during which time he managed the affairs for Chicago's La Cosa Nostra. He also operated out of Hollywood and Las Vegas, and the FBI believed he was connected with at least thirteen murders.

Roselli was involved with one of the CIA's first assassination attempts on Fidel Castro, just prior to the Bay of Pigs incident. Two CIA agents, William Harvey and James O'Connell, accompanied Roselli to Miami, where they recruited a Cuban native who was related to one of Castro's chefs. Their plan was to lace the dictator's food with a drug that would take three days to kill him, by which time any trace of the drug would have dissipated. In early 1961, a report was published in newspapers that Castro was ill, but there was no word of how serious his condition was. It was clear, however, that Castro was still alive.

Another early attempt involved a young woman named Marita Lorenz who would become Castro's lover, later recruited by the agency to be Fidel's femme fatale. Lorenz and her family immigrated to the United States in 1950. Her father captained small cruise ships, and Lorenz was working on one of her father's ships, the *Berlin*, in 1959, when it pulled into Havana harbor. A boat soon appeared and approached the *Berlin*. One man out of the twenty-seven-man crew aboard the launch stood on the bow with a rifle in his hand and shouted, "I want to come aboard!" It was Fidel Castro.

"This is a German ship!" Marita shouted at Castro, to which the Cuban leader replied, "Yes, but you are in my harbor." In many interviews following that first encounter, Lorenz said she was immediately mesmerized by Castro. That night, the two had dinner, and she fell in love.

A few days later, the *Berlin* returned to its home port in New York. Marita received a phone call the following day. It was Castro, informing her that he was sending his private jet to pick her up and return her to Havana.

Lorenz lived with Castro for several months at his headquarters in the Habana Libre Hotel. She eventually became pregnant with Castro's child. In October 1959, Marita was sitting at a table drinking a glass of milk when she realized that she had been slipped a Mickey. She had been drugged. Had she accidentally taken a drink from a glass meant for Castro?

Lorenz passed out. The next thing she knew, she awoke in a hospital. Groggy from the drug, she was informed by doctors that the baby had to be "taken away because of Fidel's enemies." She was flown back to New York, where she was treated at Roosevelt Hospital. The young woman had barely survived a botched abortion that had been performed on the island.

While recuperating in the hospital, she had her first meeting with FBI agents Frank O'Brien and Frank Lundquist. After reliving her experience of the past few days, she told the agents that she no longer loved Castro and had "turned against him." The meeting ended, and before she knew it, she was being contacted by the CIA.

The agency had her contact Castro and arrange a meeting with him. Castro agreed, and the agency flew her back to Cuba. Lorenz had brought two botulinum toxin capsules with her, planning to drop them into Castro's drink, killing him in thirty seconds. She had hidden the capsules in a jar of cold cream, where no one would find them. There were two problems, however: First, the cold cream dissolved the pills, rendering them useless; and second, she had reconsidered and could not complete the mission.

When she arrived at Castro's room, he lay on the bed, chewing his famous cigar. "Did you come here to kill me?" he asked. She casually replied, "I wanted to see you." Leaning over, Castro pulled out a .45 caliber pistol from a drawer and handed it to Lorenz. Without flinching, he said to her, "You can't kill me. Nobody can kill me."

She had fallen into Castro's spell once again. The pair made love, and afterward, Castro left the room and she never saw him again. Meanwhile in New York, the CIA was listening to a radio and heard Castro give a speech. They knew that Marita Lorenz had not accomplished her mission. Upon her return to New York, an unidentified agent walked up to her and said, "Now we've gotta go to war because of you." Shortly afterwards, the failed Bay of Pigs Invasion occurred.

Those were the first two attempts to assassinate Castro, but they were far from the last. According to a Senate subcommittee account known as the Church Report, released in 1976, and a book written by CIA operative Fabian Escalante, who had inside knowledge of events, there were 634 attempts to assassinate Fidel Castro. Some of the plans appeared to be straight out of a James Bond novel, while others were laughable at best.

Several attempts to kill Castro involved one of his many vices. The dictator was well known for loving his big Cuban cigars. Virtually every photograph taken of him portrays Castro with a large stogie clenched between his teeth. The CIA went out of their way to prove, at least in Castro's case, that smoking is bad for your health when they laced a box of cigars with enough botulinum toxin that simply putting the smoke between your lips would kill you. The box of cigars was supposed to be delivered to the Cuban dictator by an unidentified individual during a 1961 United Nations meeting in New York. The box never arrived, and no one knows what happened to the smokes.

Another cigar plan almost looks like it came from a Three Stooges short. In any good novelty store, one can purchase an exploding cigar. Hand the cigar to an unsuspecting target, light it, and the end blows off harmlessly. It's just a loud "snap" like a cap gun going off. The CIA had other plans, rigging a box of the dictator's cigars with enough explosive material that when one was lit, it would blow Castro's head off. Historians are still debating whether this exploding cigar plan is urban legend or the truth.

Two other plans that were definitely true involved using another one of Fidel Castro's favorite pastimes to kill him: scuba diving in the warm, brilliant blue Caribbean waters. The agency spent a considerable amount of money and time to locate a large Caribbean mollusk big enough to conceal an explosive device. The exploding shell would be painted brilliant colors to catch Castro's eye, and when he went to investigate it, it would explode. The plan was abandoned when it was deemed "impractical," but they had something a little more nefarious up their sleeves: contaminating his diving gear.

The plan involved the famous US negotiator, James Donovan, remembered for his role in negotiating the release of U-2 spy plane pilot Francis Gary Powers in 1962, memorialized in the Tom Hanks movie, *Bridge of Spies*. The idea was that Donovan would present the Cuban leader with a gift of a new wet suit. The CIA would line the inside with a fungus that would cause the highly debilitating disease, Madura foot (mycetoma), which forms tumor-like masses beneath the skin. They would also present him with a new breathing apparatus lined with *Mycobacterium tuberculosis* (TB). Once again, the plan failed when the diving gear never left the laboratory.

There was another plan involving a ballpoint pen outfitted with a hypodermic needle so fine that when it was used, the victim wouldn't even notice the pin prick. According to testimony before the Church Committee, the CIA case officer was not impressed with the pen and called it off, saying that "surely the CIA could come up with something better than that."

One attempt was more to discredit the dictator than kill him. During an overseas trip, the CIA planned to wait incognito near

Castro's hotel room. When he put his shoes outside of his room to be shined, the agency would coat the inside of the shoes with thallium salts, a drug that in low amounts would cause excessive vomiting, diarrhea, and, as the CIA hoped, a loss of hair, in particular his famous beard, which would cause him great embarrassment. Oh, and there was a chance that if a large-enough amount were used, it could result in his death, a bonus in the eyes of the CIA. Once again, the plan was thwarted when the unknowing Castro canceled his trip.

The closest anyone ever came to killing Castro occurred in 1963. Once again, the agency's favorite poison, botulinum toxin, would be the means to off the dictator, and this time, it would be placed in his favorite beverage, a chocolate milkshake. Two mobsters, Salvatore Giancana and Santo Trafficante Jr., would do the honors.

The pair arrived in Havana in March 1963, setting up shop in the Habana Libre Hotel, where Castro lived and worked. They successfully smuggled the pills into the hotel restaurant's freezer for safekeeping and just had to wait for the right moment to slip them into Castro's milkshake. When the time arrived, a hotel waiter who had been recruited into the plot went to the freezer to retrieve the pills. Once again, there was a problem. The pills had frozen on the shelf, and when the waiter attempted to remove them, the capsules tore open and spilled out onto the floor.

Meanwhile, out in the restaurant, Castro was handed his milkshake and sipped on it serenely as Giancana and Trafficante could only sit and watch.

In the end, after 634 attempts to assassinate Fidel Castro (167 of those during the Kennedy administration), Castro, the man with more lives than a cat, wound up dying of natural causes in 2016, at the age of ninety.

FOOTNOTE TO HISTORY:
A LETTER TO THE PRESIDENT

When Fidel Castro took control of the Cuban government in 1958, the CIA and the State Department went into high gear, profiling their nearest communist neighbor. Their conclusion was that while Castro had a high intellect, he was also a narcissist, thinking highly of himself and thriving on praise from those around him. It was a trait that the United States would attempt to capitalize on over the many years they attempted to assassinate the Cuban leader.

When Castro was a boy, like many inquisitive youngsters, he decided to write a letter to the president of the United States, Franklin Roosevelt, just weeks after FDR was reelected for his fourth term in office. The letter is part of a collection held by the National Archives, an unusual piece of history buried away among the millions of historic documents preserved there. Although Fidel states that he is twelve in the letter, the date reveals that he was actually fourteen years old when he wrote it. Was the youngster a fan of Roosevelt, or was he trying to make a quick buck? Maybe, it was a little of both.

In very broken English, Castro begins with an odd greeting: "My good friend Roosevelt." From there, he congratulates the president on his reelection. "I like to hear the radio, and I am very happy, because I heard in it that you will be President for a new *periodo* [Spanish for "period"]." Then, the letter makes a request:

If you like, give me a ten dollars bill green American in the letter, because never I have not seen a ten dollars green American and I would like to have one of them.

An unusual request for a fourteen-year-old boy, but then again, weren't we all trying to make some money to buy a comic book or two at that age? Either way, it was an unusual request, the first time—but far from the last—that Fidel Castro would write to an American president.

· 21 ·

COME FLY WITH ME . . .
TO THE MOON

In an episode of the hit American Movie Classics (AMC) television series, *Mad Men*, which focuses on a prestigious advertising agency in New York City in the early 1960s, the main character, Don Draper—played by actor Jon Hamm—is seen previewing a marketing campaign for the Hilton Hotel chain to the company's president, Conrad Hilton. In the scene, Draper is standing in front of an easel, reading each proposed ad, flipping through the cards one by one until he comes to the end of his presentation.

"There is one word that promises the thrill of international travel and the comfort of home," Draper says, before launching into a series of rhetorical questions which he answers himself. "How do you say 'ice water' in Italian? Hilton. How do you say 'fresh towels' in Farsi? Hilton. How do you say 'hamburger' in Japanese? Hilton."

Hilton leans back in his chair, takes a deep breath, and says, "It's good. Very good. It's clever and friendly, yet draws you in. But what about the moon?"

Draper is confused. "Excuse me?"

"There's nothing about the moon," Hilton says.

"Well," Draper says, still taken aback by Hilton's question, "that's not an actual destination."

"That wasn't the point," Hilton replies. "I said I wanted Hilton on the moon. I couldn't have been more clear about it."

Wait. Hold on. Rewind. The moon? Sounds like something only a writer could think up, right? Well, it wasn't.

While the scene may have been fictional, in 1967, Hilton was actually talking about putting a Hilton Hotel in Earth's orbit and on the moon, even though it would be another two years before humans would orbit our nearest celestial neighbor, and another three years before the first men landed on the moon. They even went so far as to have conceptual drawings designed for what he called the Lunar Hilton. While Conrad Hilton first came up with the idea of a futuristic hotel, it would be his son, Barron, who would actually draw up the plans.

Barron Hilton was born in Dallas, Texas, on October 23, 1927, the second oldest of Conrad Hilton's three children. By this time, the family patriarch was already making a name for himself in the hotel industry, having opened his first, the Mobley Hotel, in Cisco, Texas, in 1919. From there, he slowly began building his empire by buying more and more hotels throughout Texas in the years that followed. The family eventually moved to Los Angeles where Conrad opened another hotel, called the Townhouse. When young Barron became a teenager, his father gave him his first hotel-related job, parking cars.

From an early age Barron had yearned to fly, and at seventeen, he obtained a pilot's license. Before fully immersing himself in the family business, the young Hilton went off to war, serving as a navy photographer during World War II. Upon his discharge, Barron made a name for himself in business, acquiring the Vita-Pakt Juice Company; founding the first aircraft-leasing company, Air Finance; and creating the Carte Blanche credit card company. Hilton also became the owner of the Los Angeles Chargers football team, which later became the San Diego Chargers when it moved to the Southern California city.

In 1954, Barron Hilton was named the vice president of the hotel chain, and in 1966, he was offered the position of president and CEO of Hilton Hotels, succeeding his father. Selling his ownership of the Chargers, Barron Hilton took over the reins of the chain. The company saw remarkable growth during the ensuing years, when Barron allowed the Hilton brand to be franchised.

The idea for a space-based Hilton actually began years earlier when rumors about such an endeavor began spreading through the press in 1957, after Conrad Hilton held an event at his swanky Conrad Hilton Hotel in Chicago. The extravaganza featured a floor show with astronaut-themed dancers high-stepping across a stage, decked out with futuristic space-related backdrops. Newspapers began circulating the story that the elder Hilton was going big with a moon-based Hilton. Chicago's *Suburbanite Economist* wrote of the event, saying that the dancers were prancing through a "plush Lunar Hilton." In 1963, *Cosmopolitan* magazine did a profile of the elder Hilton, writing, "It won't be long before our astronauts land on the moon and immediately behind them will be Connie Hilton with his plans for the Lunar Hilton Hotel."

Fast-forward to 1967, when Barron, now fully in charge of the Hilton chain, told the *Wall Street Journal* that he could see a Lunar Hilton being constructed in his lifetime. While Barron knew that such a vision would take years, if not decades or more, to become a reality, he went ahead and ordered drawings and sketches made up of what his vision could look like.

For the Earth-orbiting Hilton, Barron envisioned a circular space-station design that closely resembled the one famed rocket scientist Wernher von Braun presented on an episode of the *Disneyland* television show, titled "Man in Space." The ring would spin slowly in space, giving occupants the feeling of gravity. The hotel would have three levels and one hundred rooms for visitors who wanted to stay for a short holiday, or just spend a night before heading to the moon.

The Lunar Hilton was much more ambitious. It would be built 30 feet under the lunar surface to stabilize the extreme temperatures on the moon. There would be three floors: the lower level would hold the mechanics that would keep oxygen flowing throughout the complex, as well as electrical and heating systems, and so forth. The second level would consist of two 400-foot-long corridors that would be connected by airlocks and accommodate one hundred people. The upper level near the surface of the moon would house the main lobby, dining room, and the cocktail lounge. When presenting the Lunar Hilton concept to the American Astronautical Society in 1967, Barron told those gathered, "If you think we are not going to have a cocktail lounge, you don't know Hilton."

To promote the hotel chain and to get people excited about what the future held for the hotel in the not-too-distant future, Hilton had some swag made up for current customers, including mock room keys with the words LUNAR HILTON emblazoned on them, to be handed out to guests when they checked into their Earth-bound hotel rooms. They also printed and distributed promotional reservation cards that offered single, double, or cloud suite rooms, and the option of taking an "Intergalactic Express" ride to the moon, all with the caveat that arrival dates "must be after 1980."

Of course, the dream of a Lunar Hilton never saw the light of day—but hold on a second. A new private company, Voyager Space, is one of several companies contracted by NASA to launch new generations of space stations into Earth's orbit, to replace the International Space Station when it is finally decommissioned in 2030. The company's *Starlab* space station will provide greater opportunities for scientists and researchers to explore new manufacturing processes in pharmaceuticals, biology, and more. Of course, these researchers will need a place to lay their heads after an exhausting day at work. Enter Hilton Hotels, who has signed an agreement to build crew accommodation and communal areas aboard *Starlab*. While not the same hotel envisioned by Conrad and Barron Hilton, it will be the first step toward that goal.

The dream of an orbiting station or building a moon-based Hilton Hotel depends on the ability to send average, everyday people reliably and safely into space. On July 21, 2021, this next step in human space travel was taken when billionaire Jeff Bezos successfully launched the first all-civilian crew of private citizens into space. The fifteen-minute suborbital flight, much like those taken by NASA's *Mercury* astronauts in the early 1960s, included Bezos, his brother Mark, Oliver Daemen (a paying customer), and Mary Wallace "Wally" Funk. In 2021, Funk was the last surviving member of the *Mercury 13* group, and one of the First Lady Astronaut Trainees (FLATs). The FLATs underwent the same physical and mental tests that the male *Mercury* astronauts were subjected to in the 1960s, but were denied the opportunity to fly into space for a variety of reasons, one of which was simply their gender.

During a post-flight press conference, Bezos was asked by reporters how it felt. "Wonder how it felt?" he excitedly replied. "*Oh my God!* My expectations were high, and they were dramatically exceeded. The most profound piece of it for me was looking out at the Earth and looking at the Earth's atmosphere. Every astronaut, everybody who has been up into space, says that it changes them. They are kind of amazed and awestruck by the Earth and its beauty, but also its fragility. And I can vouch for that."

It was the opening of a new era. Commercial space travel was becoming a reality. Granted, the flight of the *New Shepard* was only a brief fifteen-minute ride into the lower reaches of space, and the crew was only weightless for a total of three minutes. Nevertheless, it was a monumental achievement: Civilians had been launched into space by a private company. Steps were being taken to make spaceflight as commonplace as flying in an airliner.

Once the *New Shepard* had landed in a west Texas desert, the debate began: Should private industry be allowed to conduct such trips into space? After all, this is one of the most dangerous jobs in the world, climbing aboard what could ostensibly be called a giant stick of dynamite that puts the crew, engineers, and spectators at risk should anything go wrong. On the second flight of the *New Shepard*, actor William Shatner, best known for his role as captain of the USS *Enterprise* in the television series *Star Trek*, was aboard. Could you imagine the outcry if Captain Kirk had been blown up?

As with all new ventures, there are two sides to the story. Yes, it is a dangerous industry that should be regulated to keep everyone safe, but then again, isn't this how the airline industry began? Visionary inventors and eccentric billionaires pushing the envelope of air travel to make it accessible, first to the wealthy, and then to the general public?

Decades before Bezos and Virgin Galactic's owner Richard Branson (who is also building a commercial spaceship) dreamed of sending civilians to the stars, and about the same time Barron Hilton began dreaming of a Hilton Hotel on the moon, another company was already making plans to send average, everyday people to a destination where "no one had gone before"—the moon. Well, that's not quite right. They were not really planning on sending travelers to the moon, but it became quite the marketing scheme. What started as a small joke by a random newspaper reporter in Austria quickly became a marketing campaign for the largest worldwide airline, and as with Barron Hilton's dream of building a lunar hotel, it happened in the early days of the Space Age.

Sometime in 1964, an Austrian journalist, Gerhard Pistor, walked into a Viennese travel agency to reserve a seat on a very special flight. Pistor calmly stepped up to the travel agent and requested a reservation on a flight to the moon. Needless to say, the agent was quite surprised by his request. Knowing full well there were no such flights, and none planned in the near future, the ticket agent dutifully performed their job and sent the journalist's request to the Pan American Airlines reservation office.

At the time, Pan American was the principal international airline of the United States. The first routes flown by the airline began in 1927, when their fleet of small airplanes would fly mail from Key West, Florida, to Havana, Cuba. One year later, and under the technical direction of famed aviator Charles Lindbergh, the airline began expanding its routes, adding passenger service to Buenos Aires, and then to Chile. By 1937, Pan Am had added transatlantic routes.

From that moment on, Pan American World Airlines, as it was now called, became the leader in international air travel, which had expanded even further to include around-the-world routes. By the 1970s, airline deregulation allowed other airlines to begin international service, and Pan Am started facing financial difficulties. By the end of that decade, the company was trying in vain to get back to its roots by introducing domestic service in the United States. The company even went so far as to sell its international routes to other airlines to infuse much-needed cash into the business, but it was too late; the writing was on the wall, and the company filed for bankruptcy in 1991. Still, throughout the 1960s, Pan Am was the go-to for international travel, so a request for a ticket to the moon was almost, and I stress *almost*, reasonable. That is, except for the fact that no one had flown to the moon yet.

After asking for a ticket to the moon, Pistor returned home disappointed (one would imagine) that he couldn't take his out-of-this-world vacation. Two weeks later, Pistor was surprised when he received a letter from Pan Am informing him that his reservation had been accepted and that he could expect the first flight to the moon to occur sometime in the year 2000.

As it turns out, Pistor's request gave the airline fodder to create a brilliant marketing scheme—the Pan Am First Moon Flights Club. While it was just a gimmick, it kept the airline's name in front of the public's eyes, and soon, people were flooding the airline with requests for a reservation.

To join the club, you simply had to send a letter to the company with your name and address; in return, you would receive an official card free of charge in the mail. The cards were sequentially numbered, so potential passengers would be prioritized in proper order when flights were finally available and ticket reservations could be made. A letter accompanying the card made it clear that "fares are not fully resolved and may be out of this world." Oh, and the cards were nontransferable.

You're probably thinking this was a clever ploy by Pan Am to add names to their contact list for promotional use, but representatives of Pan Am at the time staunchly defended the program, saying that flying people to the moon would eventually happen, and the airline would be the first to do it. Reading between the lines—it was a ploy to get names into their sales database.

In 1968, the First Moon Flights Club had an unexpected boost from an incredibly successful science-fiction movie, Stanley Kubrick's *2001: A Space Odyssey*. As the movie begins, a spaceship named *Orion III* is shown slowly approaching a rotating space station shuttling people to orbit from Earth. Emblazoned on the side of the spacecraft was the iconic blue-and-white Pan Am logo. The spacecraft and logo were also immortalized on the famous poster created for the movie by painter Robert McCall.

Before Pan Am went bankrupt in 1991, over 90,000 people had become members of the First Moon Flights Club. The list included the likes of former US senator and presidential candidate Barry Goldwater, California governor and future US president Ronald Reagan, and journalist Walter Cronkite. And while the cards can no longer be redeemed (sorry, still no scheduled commercial flights to the moon), the cards have gained value, both monetarily, as a collector's item, and sentimentally, as a source of nostalgia for early space history.

FOOTNOTE TO HISTORY: AVOIDING A CONSPIRACY THEORY—NUKE THE MOON

It's hard to believe that more than fifty years since Neil Armstrong became the first man to walk on the moon during the flight of *Apollo 11*, 10 percent of Americans polled still believe the moon landings were staged, nothing but a hoax. The conspiracy theory has been going around since the flight of *Apollo 11* ended, so much so that the second man to walk on the moon, Buzz Aldrin, when confronted by a naysayer, socked the man in the nose.

The funny thing is that during the early days of spaceflight in the late 1950s, after launching the world's first satellite, *Sputnik 1*, the Soviet Union was looking far into the future and dreaming of a landing on the moon. The incredible advances in rocketry and space exploration by the Russians in the late 1950s and early 1960s gave them the motivation to push on with their goal of being the first country to land a man on the moon. The scientists realized their mission might be deemed a hoax, however, because at the time, there was no way of proving they had actually landed there. Telemetry data and tracking during this era, as well as the fact that early television signals could not make the journey, made this a real possibility.

Enter Russian rocket scientist Boris Chertok, who had an idea to prove they had landed: nuke the moon. Chertok's plan was to have the first cosmonauts on the moon detonate an atom bomb near their landing site. Astronomers on Earth would see the brilliant nuclear flash, which would signify to the world that the cosmonauts had made it safely.

There were a couple of issues with this theory. First, some scientists worried that a nuclear explosion would rip the moon out of Earth's orbit, causing global destruction, much like what occurred in the old 1970s TV series, *Space: 1999*. Oh, and then there's the fact that the moon has no atmosphere, meaning the expected hellish red glow and mushroom cloud would not happen. The bomb would only leave yet another small crater on the moon's surface.

The plan was quietly abandoned.

ACKNOWLEDGMENTS

I couldn't have written this book without the valuable input of all those who have helped make it possible. My deepest thanks go to Valerie Ellis and the staff of the Mobile Public Library, particularly those in the Local History and Genealogy department; to Dr. Greg Waselkov, professor emeritus of anthropology at the University of South Alabama; to Mike Bunn, author, historian, and director of Blakeley Historic State Park; to historian and author John Sledge; to the historians and curators at the Scituate Historical Society; to Tom McAnear, with the National Archives; to Laura Secord, the great-great-great-granddaughter of Laura Ingersoll Secord; and of course, as always, to my wife Maggie, for her patience as I waded through another project, squawking day in and day out about little tidbits of history I uncovered for this book.

BIBLIOGRAPHY

Chapter 1: The Pig War

Coleman, E. E. *Pig War: The Most Perfect War in History*. Stroud, England: The History Press, 2009.

National Park Service. "San Juan Island National Historical Park Washington: The Pig War." National Park Service, May 23, 2023. Accessed April 2, 2024. https://www.nps.gov/sajh/learn/historyculture/the-pig-war.htm.

Neering, Rosemary. *The Pig War: The Last Canada–U.S. Border Conflict*. British Columbia: Heritage House Publishing, 2011.

Sainsbury, Brendan. "The US Island That Nearly Ignited a War." BBC, September 12, 2022. Accessed April 2, 2024. https://www.bbc.com/travel/article/20220911-the-us-island-that-nearly-ignited-a-war.

Vouri, Mike. *The Pig War: Standoff at Griffin Bay*. Seattle, WA: Discover Your Northwest, 1999.

———. *The Pig War*. Mount Pleasant, SC: Arcadia Publishing, 2008.

Chapter 2: The Tale of the Pelican Girls

Bunn, Mike. Director, Historic Blakeley State Park. In discussion with the author, April 2024.

Ellis, Valerie. Local History & Genealogy, Mobile Public Library. In discussion with the author, March 2024.

Hamilton, Peter J. *Colonial Mobile: An Historical Study Largely from Original Sources of the Alabama-Tombigbee Basin from the Discovery of Mobile Bay in 1519 Until the Demolition of Fort Charlotte in 1821*. Boston: Houston, Mifflin, and Company, 1897.

"History of the French Caribbean: Woman from Martinique, 'potomitan.'" Accessed February 20, 2024. https://azmartinique.com/en/all-to-know/studies-research/history-of-the-french-caribbean-woman-from-martinique-the-poto-mitan#toc-the-settler-s-wife-the-wife-of-elite-society.

Jones, Terry L. "A Shortage of Women: Wives Are Imported, Acorns Are Eaten, and, Naturally, a Petticoat Rebellion Follows." *Country Roads Magazine*, August 16, 2017. https://countryroadsmagazine.com/art-and-culture/history/a-shortage-of-women/.

Kazek, Kelly. "When French Orphans Called Casket Girls Came to Alabama as Wives for Colonists." September 14, 2015. Accessed February 20, 2024. https://www.al.com/living/2015/09/when_french_orphans_called_cas.html.

Knight, Vernon James, and Sheree L. Adams. "A Voyage to the Mobile and Tomeh in 1700, With Notes on the Interior of Alabama." *Ethnohistory* 28, no. 2 (January 1, 1981): 179. https://doi.org/10.2307/481117.

Saucier, Wayne A. "The Pelican Girls." *Saucier Family Weebly*. Saucier Family, 2006. Accessed February 20, 2024. https://thesaucierfamily.weebly.com/the-pelican-girls.html.

Sledge, John. Historian/author, *Mobile Bay Magazine*. In discussion with the author, April 2024.

Waselkov, Gregory A. Professor emeritus of anthropology, Archaeology Department, University of South Alabama. In discussion with the author, April 2024.

Chapter 3: They Didn't Get the Memo

Andrlik, Todd, and Hugh T. Harrington. *Journal of the American Revolution, Annual Volume 2015*. Chicago: Westholme Publishing, 2015.

Chaffin, Tom. *Sea of Grey: The Around-the-World Odyssey of the Confederate Raider Shenandoah*. New York: Hill and Wang, 2006.

Cuhaj, Joe. *Hidden History of Mobile*. Charleston, SC: History Press, 2019.

———. *A History Lover's Guide to Mobile and the Alabama Gulf Coast*. Charleston, SC: History Press, 2023.

"The Great Chain across the Hudson River." Albert Wisner Public Library, Warwick, New York, February 7, 2018. Accessed March 14, 2024. https://guides.rcls.org/chain.

Harrington, Hugh T. "The Great West Point Chain." Places. *Journal of the American Revolution*, September 25, 2014. Accessed March 14, 2014. https://allthingsliberty.com/2014/09/the-great-west-point-chain/.

Levine, David. "A 75-Ton Chain Once Stretched across the Hudson to Stop the British." Hudson Valley, January 10, 2018. Accessed March 31, 2024. https://hvmag.com/life-style/hudson-valley-chain-american-revolution/.

Markowitz, Mike. "CSS *Shenandoah* and the Last Shot of the Civil War." Defense Media Network. Accessed March 14, 2024. https://www.defensemedianetwork.com/stories/how-the-rebels-saved-the-whales/.

McLachlan, Sean, and Charles River Editors. *The Battle of Palmito Ranch: The History of the Last Battle of the Civil War*. Ann Arbor, MI: Charles River Editors, 2018.

North Carolina Department of Natural and Cultural Resources. "A Civil War Surrender Six Months after Appomattox." State of North Carolina, November 6, 2016. Accessed March 14, 2024. https://www.dncr.nc.gov/blog/2016/11/06/civil-war-surrender-six-months-after-appomattox.

Remini, Robert. *The Battle of New Orleans: Andrew Jackson and America's First Military Victory*. New York: Penguin Books, 2001.

Schooler, Lynn. Last Shot: *The Incredible Story of the CSS* Shenandoah *and the True Conclusion of the Civil War*. Waterville, ME: Thorndike Press, 2005.

Smithweck, David. *Fort Bowyer: Defender of Mobile Bay, 1814–1815.* Scotts Valley, CA: CreateSpace Independent Publishing Platform, 2015.

"Soldiering On: Famous Battles Fought After the War Ended." Military History Now, January 6, 2015. Accessed March 14, 2024. https://militaryhis torynow.com/2015/01/06/soldiering-on-famous-battles-fought-after-the-war -ended-2/.

Weitz, Mark A. "Confederate Commerce Raiders and Privateers." Essential Civil War Curriculum, Virginia Center for Civil War Studies. Accessed March 14, 2024. https://www.dncr.nc.gov/blog/2016/11/06/civil-war-surrender-six -months-after-appomattox.

Chapter 4: Princess Charlotte and the Great Russian Royalty Hoax

Bunn, Mike. Director, Historic Blakeley State Park. In discussion with the author, April 2024.

Clark, Robert T. "The Fusion of Legends in Zschokke's 'Prinzessin von Wolfenbüttel.'" *Journal of English and Germanic Philology* 42, no. 2 (1943): 185–96. http://www .jstor.org/stable/27704975.

Ellis, Valerie. 2024. Local History & Genealogy, Mobile Public Library. In discussion with the author, March 2024.

Higgenbotham, Jay. *Old Mobile: Fort Louisiane, 1702–1711.* Mobile, AL: Museum of the City of Mobile, 1977.

Jones, Pam. "Mobile's Anastasia." *Alabama Heritage / University of Alabama*, Issue 78 (Fall 2005). November 21, 2018. Accessed March 2, 2024. https://www.ala bamaheritage.com/from-the-vault/mobiles-anastasia.

Sledge, John. "The Legend of Mobile's Princess Charlotte Christina Sophia." *Mobile Bay Magazine.* August 18, 2022. Accessed March 2, 2024. https://mobile baymag.com/the-legend-of-mobiles-princess-charlotte-christina-sophia/.

———. Historian/author, *Mobile Bay Magazine.* In discussion with the author, April 2024.

Waselkov, Gregory A. Professor emeritus of anthropology, Archaeology Department, University of South Alabama. In discussion with the author, April 2024.

Chapter 5: America's First Black Woman Political Writer and Abolitionist, Maria W. Stewart

"(1832) Maria W. Stewart, 'Why Sit Ye Here and Die?'" African American History Timeline. Black Past, January 24, 2007. https://www.blackpast.org /african-american-history/1832-maria-w-stewart-why-sit-ye-here-and-die/.

Garrison, W. Lloyd. *Meditations from the Pen of Maria W. Stewart.* Washington, DC: Enterprise Publishing Company, 1879.

"The Liberator (Boston, Mass.) 1831–1865." Library of Congress. Accessed March 28, 2024. https://www.loc.gov/item/sn84031524/.

"Maria Miller Stewart." Connecticut Women's Hall of Fame. Accessed March 24, 2024. https://www.cwhf.org/inductees/maria-miller-stewart.

"Maria W. Stewart." Boston African American National Historic Site. National Park Service. Accessed March 28, 2024. https://www.nps.gov/people/maria-w-stewart.htm.

Rediker, Marcus. *The Fearless Benjamin Lay: The Quaker Dwarf Who Became the First Revolutionary Abolitionist.* London: Verso-New Left Books, 2017.

Richardson, Marilyn. *Maria W. Stewart: America's First Black Woman Political Writer: Essays and Speeches (Blacks in the Diaspora).* Bloomington: Indiana University Press, 1987.

Stewart, Maria W. "Mrs. Stewart's Farewell Address to Her Friends in the City of Boston—September 21, 1833." Archives of Women's Political Communication. Iowa University. Accessed March 28, 2024. https://awpc.cattcenter.iastate.edu/2020/11/20/mrs-stewarts-farewell-address-to-her-friends-in-the-city-of-boston-sept-21-1833/.

Vaux, Roberts. *Quaker Comet: Benjamin Lay, Anti-Slavery Pioneer.* Durham, England: Langley Press, 2018.

Waters, Kristin. *Maria W. Stewart and the Roots of Political Thought.* Jackson: University Press of Mississippi, 2022.

Chapter 6: Laura Secord: War of 1812 Canadian Heroine

CBC News. "Laura Secord's Long Trek to Thwart American Invasion." Canada: The Story of Us. Canadian Broadcasting Corporation, March 20, 2017. Accessed March 24, 2024. https://www.cbc.ca/2017/canadathestoryofus/laura-secord-s-long-trek-to-thwart-american-invasion-1.4031841.

Currie, Emma A. *The Story of Laura Secord and Canadian Reminiscences.* Toronto: William Briggs, 1900.

Leavey, Peggy Dymond. *Laura Secord: Heroine of the War of 1812.* Toronto: Dundurn, 2012.

Mark, Janis. "The Hartford Convention and the Spectre of Secession." *UConn Today.* University of Connecticut, December 15, 2014. Accessed March 24, 2024. https://today.uconn.edu/2014/12/the-hartford-convention-and-the-specter-of-secession/.

McKenzie, Ruth. *Laura Secord: Legend and Lady.* Ontario: McClelland and Stewart, 1977.

National Park Service. "Summer 1813: A Dangerous Journey to Warn the British." National Park Service, September 14, 2017. Accessed April 2, 2024. https://www.nps.gov/articles/laura-secord-dangerous-journey.htm.

Ragusea, Adam. *Radio Boston.* "Why New England Almost Seceded over the War of 1812." June 15, 2012, WBUR. https://www.wbur.org/radioboston/2012/06/15/new-england-succession.

Chapter 7: The Two-Girl Army

D'Entremont, Jeremy. "History of Scituate Light, Massachusetts." New England Lighthouses, a Virtual Guide. Accessed May 17, 2024. http://www.newengland lighthouses.net/scituate-light-history.html.

Freitas, Fred. *Humarock Hummocks, Humming Rocks, and Silver Sands.* Scituate, MA: Scituate Historical Society, 2019.

Morgan, Winifred. *An American Icon: Brother Jonathan and American Identity.* Newark: University of Delaware Press, 1988.

"National Symbols, Stories & Icons." Star Spangled Banner. National Park Service, April 7, 2020. Accessed March 31, 2024. https://www.nps.gov/stsp/learn/his toryculture/national-symbols-stories-icons.htm#:~:text=Library%20of%20 Congress-,Uncle%20Sam,Uncle%20Sam%E2%80%9D%E2%80%94was%20 invented.

Porter, Mary. Scituate Historical Society. In discussion with the author, April 2024.

"Scituate 1811, Book 116, page 182. "Scituate Lighthouse, Rebecca and Abigail Bates, American Army of Two." Notable Land Records. Plymouth County Registry of Deeds. Accessed March 31, 2024. https://www.plymouthdeeds.org /sites/g/files/vyhlif4881/f/file/file/rebecca-and-abigail-bates-army-of-two.pdf.

Scituate Historical Society. "Scituate Lighthouse, 1810." Scituate Historical Society, May 17, 2021. Accessed March 31, 2024. https://scituatehistoricalsociety.org /historic_property/scituate-lighthouse/.

———. Director, Historic Blakeley State Park. In discussion with the author, April 2024.

Wood, Allen. "Daughters of Keeper Save Scituate Lighthouse during War of 1812." New England Lighthouse Stories. September 1, 2020. Accessed May 17, 2024. https://www.nelights.com/blog/daughters-of-keeper-save-scituate-light house-during-war-of-1812/.

Chapter 8: The Free States of . . .

Barksdale, Kevin. "The Creation of West Virginia." *Encyclopedia of Virginia.* Virginia Humanities, June 21, 2023. Accessed May 1, 2024. https://encyclopediavirginia .org/entries/west-virginia-creation-of/.

Census.Gov. "Mapping Slavery in the Nineteenth Century." National Oceanic and Atmospheric Administration (NOAA). Accessed May 1, 2024. https://www .census.gov/history/pdf/slavedensitymap.pdf.

Eastman, Margaret Middleton Rivers. *Hidden History of Civil War Charleston.* Charleston, SC: History Press, 2012.

Fontenay, Blake. "The Curious History of the 'Free and Independent State of Scott.'" *Tri Star Chronicles.* Tennessee Secretary of State, January 17, 2017. Accessed April 30, 2024. https://sos.tn.gov/tsla/pages/tri-star-chronicles-scott-county.

"The Free and Independent State of Scott." Scott County, Tennessee. Scott County Chamber of Commerce. Accessed April 22, 2024. https://scottcounty.com /welcome/about-scott-county/the-free-independent-state-of-scott/.

"From Charleston: The Sinking of the Stone Fleet." *New York Times,* January 8, 1862.

Gordon, Cdr. Arthur. "The Great Stone Fleet." *Proceedings,* December 1968. https:// www.usni.org/magazines/proceedings/1968/december/great-stone-fleet.

Graham, H. S., and E. Hergesheimer. *Map of Virginia: Showing the Distribution of Its Slave Population from the Census of 1860.* [Washington: Henry S. Graham, 1861]. Map. https://www.loc.gov/item/2010586916/.

Jones, Jamie L. "The Navy's Stone Fleet." The Opinionator. *New York Times*, January 26, 2012. Accessed May 1, 2024. https://archive.nytimes.com/opinionator .blogs.nytimes.com/2012/01/26/the-navys-stone-fleet/.

Kelly, James R. "Newton Knight and the Legend of the Free State of Jones." *Mississippi History Now*. Mississippi Historical Society, April 2009. Accessed May 1, 2024. https://www.mshistorynow.mdah.ms.gov/issue/newton-knight -and-the-legend-of-the-free-state-of-jones.

Lincoln, Abraham. *Abraham Lincoln Papers: Series 1. General Correspondence. 1833– 1916: Abraham Lincoln, March 1861, First Inaugural Address, Final Version*. March 1861. Manuscript/Mixed Material. https://www.loc.gov/item/mal0773800/.

Rice, Otis. *West Virginia: A History*. Lexington: University of Kentucky Press, 1985.

"The Stone Blockade." *New York Times*, November 23, 1861.

"West Virginia Statehood, June 20, 1863." The Center for Legislative Archives. National Archives. Accessed April 22, 2024. https://www.archives.gov/legisla tive/features/west-virginia.

Wills, Matthew. "Emancipation Comes to West Virginia." Daily JSTOR. JSTOR, February 14, 2023. Accessed April 1, 2024. https://daily.jstor.org /emancipation-comes-to-west-virginia/.

Chapter 9: Canada and the American Civil War

"American Civil War and Canada." The Canadian Encyclopedia. Historica Canada, June 2, 2022. Accessed April 15, 2024. https://www.thecanadianencyclopedia .ca/en/article/american-civil-war.

Ashburton. "The St. Albans Raid: The Examination at St. Johns." *New York Times*, October 27, 1864. Accessed April 15, 2024. https://timesmachine.nytimes.com /timesmachine/1864/10/27/78732999.html?pageNumber=1.

Blake, John. "She Was a Soldier—and Other Strange Civil War Stories." *CNN. com*, April 13, 2011. Accessed March 30, 2024. http://www.cnn.com/2011 /US/04/12/civil.war.strange/index.html.

Blanton, Dianne. "Women Soldiers of the Civil War." *National Archives: Prologue Magazine* 25, no. 1 (Spring 1993). https://www.archives.gov/publications/pro logue/1993/spring/women-in-the-civil-war-1.html.

Boyko, John. *Blood and Daring: How Canada Fought the American Civil War and Forged a Nation*. Toronto: Vintage Canada, 2013.

Edmonds, Emma E. *Nurse and Spy in the Union Army: The Adventures and Experiences of a Woman in Hospitals, Camps, and Battlefields*. Hartford, CT: W. S. Williams & Co., 1865.

Forsyth, John. "Free Speech or Sedition: Clement L. Vallandigham and the Copperheads, 1860–1864." Master's thesis, James Madison University, 2020. https://com mons.lib.jmu.edu/cgi/viewcontent.cgi?article=1012&context=masters202029.

"The Great American, What Is It? Chased by Copperheads." Photo, Print, Drawing. Library of Congress. Accessed April 15, 2024. https://www.loc.gov /item/2008661651/.

Home-Douglas, Pierre. "Raising Hell in Montreal: How a Ragtag Band of Confederates Made Montreal Its Base during the American Civil War." *The*

Beaver (April–May 2014). https://www.canadashistoryarchive.ca/canadas-his tory/canadas-history-apr-may-2014/flipbook/36/.

MacDonald, Cheryl. "Gilbert McMicken, Spymaster: Canada's Secret Police." *The Beaver* (June–July 1991). https://www.canadashistoryarchive.ca/canadas -history/the-beaver-jun-jul-1991/flipbook/44/.

"News from Washington: The Canadian Passports." *New York Times*, March 9, 1865. Accessed April 15, 2024. https://www.nytimes.com/1865/03/09/archives/news -from-washington-special-dispatches-to-the-newyork-times.html.

"Purpose of the Vermont Raid." *New York Times*, October 24, 1864. Accessed April 15, 2024. https://www.nytimes.com/1864/10/24/archives/purpose-of-the-ver mont-raid.html.

Rodgers, Thomas E. "Copperheads or a Respectable Minority: Current Approaches to the Study of Civil War–Era Democrats." *Indiana Magazine of History* 109, no. 2 (2013): 114–46. https://doi.org/10.5378/indimagahist.109.2.0114.

Tyrell, Jeff. "When Johnny (Canuck) Comes Marching Home Again: Canadians in the American Civil War, 1861–1865." National Defence and the Canadian Armed Forces. *Canadian Military Journal*, December 12, 2019. http://www .journal.forces.gc.ca/vol20/no1/PDF/CMJ201Ep40.pdf.

Weber, Jennifer L. *Copperheads: The Rise and Fall of Lincoln's Opponents in the North*, 1st edition. New York: Oxford University Press, 2006.

———. Weber, Jennifer L. "Lincoln's Critics: The Copperheads." *Journal of the Abraham Lincoln Association*, vol. 32, no. 1 (Winter 2011): 33–47. https:// quod.lib.umich.edu/j/jala/2629860.0032.105/—lincoln-s-critics-the-copper heads?rgn=main;view=fulltext.

Whyte, George H. "Confederate Operations in Canada during the Civil War." Master's thesis, independently published, Montreal, 2022.

Chapter 10: The Great Civil War Bread Riots

Ashcraft, Jenny. "April 2, 1863: The Richmond Bread Riot." Newspapers.com. April 1, 2021. Accessed March 1, 2024. https://blog.newspapers.com /april-2-1863-the-richmond-bread-riot/.

Bergeron, Arthur W. *Confederate Mobile*. Baton Rouge: Louisiana State University Press, January 1, 1991.

"The Bread Riots at Mobile." *Daily Missouri Democrat*, St. Louis, Missouri, October 6, 1863.

"The Bread Riots in Mobile: Two Outbreaks in One Day." *New York Times*, October 1, 1863.

Brill, Kristen. *The Weaker Sex in War: Gender and Nationalism in Civil War Virginia*. Charlottesville: University of Virginia Press, 2022.

Chesson, Michael B. "Harlots or Heroines? A New Look at the Richmond Bread Riot." *Virginia Magazine of History and Biography* 92, no. 2 (1984): 131–75. http://www.jstor.org/stable/4248710.

DeCredico, Mary. "Bread Riot, Richmond." *Encyclopedia of Virginia*, University of Virginia. Accessed March 1, 2024. https://encyclodpediavirginia.org/entries /bread-riot-richmond/.

"Great Bread Riot in Richmond: Distress and Destitution Among the People." *Lancaster Examiner*, Lancaster, Pennsylvania, April 15, 1863.

Mahr, Michael. "Feeling the Effects of Rebellion: The Virginia Bread Riots." National Museum of Civil War Medicine. November 27, 2023. Accessed March 1, 2024. https://www.civilwarmed.org/feeling-the-effects-of-rebellion -the-virginia-bread-riots/.

Massey, Mary Elizabeth. "The Food and Drink Shortage on the Confederate Homefront." *North Carolina Historical Review* 26, no. 3 (1949): 306–34. http:// www.jstor.org/stable/23515975.

———. "The Effect of Shortages on the Confederate Homefront." *Arkansas Historical Quarterly* 9, no. 3 (1950): 172–93. https://doi.org/10.2307/40017226.

Titus, Katherine R. "The Richmond Bread Riot of 1863: Class, Race, and Gender in the Urban Confederacy." *Gettysburg College Journal of the Civil War Era*, vol. 2, article 6 (2011): 84–146. https://cupola.gettysburg.edu/gcjcwe/vol2/iss1/6/.

Chapter 11: There's a Mole among Us

Carney, Samantha. "Reevaluating the Pension System: The Struggles of Black Widows Following the Civil War, c. 1861–1910." *Swarthmore University Undergraduate History Journal*, vol. 3, no. 1 (2022). https://works.swarthmore .edu/cgi/viewcontent.cgi?article=1066&context=suhj.

Fox, Alex. "The Last Person to Receive a Civil War Pension Dies at Age 90." *Smithsonian Magazine*. Smithsonian Museum, June 8, 2020. Accessed March 1, 2024. https://www.smithsonianmag.com/smart-news/last-person-receive -civil-war-pension-dies-180975049/.

Good, Cassandra. "Comb through This Collection of Presidential Hair." At the Smithsonian. *Smithsonian Magazine*, February 9, 2016. Accessed March 1, 2024. https://www.smithsonianmag.com/smithsonian-institution/comb -through-framed-collection-presidential-hair-180958064/.

Gorman, Kathleen L. "Civil War Pensions." Essential Civil War Curriculum. Virginia Tech, Accessed March 1, 2024. https://www.essentialcivilwarcurric ulum.com/civil-war-pensions.html.

"Hair of the Presidents." National Museum of American History Behring Center. Smithsonian Institute. Accessed March 1, 2024. https://americanhistory.si.edu /collections/nmah_524091.

HParkins. "Weird but True." Pieces of History. National Archives, November 12, 2010. Accessed March 1, 2024. https://prologue.blogs.archives.gov/tag /weird-but-true/.

———. "The Must-Have Christmas Gift of 1864." Pieces of History. National Archives, November 16, 2010. Accessed March 1, 2024. https://prologue.blogs .archives.gov/2010/11/16/the-must-have-christmas-gift-of-1864/.

———. "The Real Widows of the Pension Office." Pieces of History. National Archives, October 15, 2012. Accessed March 1, 2024. https://prologue.blogs .archives.gov/2012/10/15/the-real-widows-of-the-pension-office/.

Hunter, Alfred. *Popular Catalogue of the Extraordinary Curiosities in the National Institute*. Washington, DC: 1856.

National Archives Museum. "Featured Document: Want to Search for the Yeti?" National Archives, November 6, 2020. Accessed March 15, 2024. https://mu seum.archives.gov/featured-document-want-hunt-yeti.

Prechtel-Kluskens, Claire. "A Reasonable Degree of Promptitude: Civil War Pension Application Processing, 1861–1865." *Prologue Magazine*, vol. 42, no. 1 (Spring 2010). https://www.archives.gov/publications/prologue/2010/spring/civil warpension.

Salisbury, Laura. "Union Army Widows and the Historical Take-up of Social Benefits." Department of Economics, York University. National Bureau of Economic Research. Accessed March 1, 2024. https://www.nber.org/system /files/chapters/c14846/c14846.pdf.

"United States, Civil War Widows and Other Dependents Pension Files—Family Search Historical Records." Family Search, January 8, 2024. Accessed March 15, 2024. https://www.familysearch.org/en/wiki/United_States,_Civil_War _Widows_and_Other_Dependents_Pension_Files_-_FamilySearch_Histori cal_Records#:~:text=A%20widow%20also%20had%20to,These%20records%20 are%20generally%20accurate.

Chapter 12: Slaves Can Be Free . . . Just Not Here

Adams, Carl. *Nance: Trials of the First Slave Freed by Abraham Lincoln: A True Story of Nance Legins-Costley*. New York: Shakespeare & Co., 2014.

"The African American Mosaic: Colonization." Exhibitions. Library of Congress, July 23, 2010. Accessed April 14, 2024. https://www.loc.gov/exhibits/african /afam002.html.

Bunn, Mike. Director, Historic Blakeley State Park. In discussion with the author, April 2024.

Cassie, Ron. "Decades Before the Civil War, Maryland Funded a Colony in Liberia to 'Resettle' Free African Americans." *Baltimore Magazine* (February 2024). https://www.baltimoremagazine.com/section/historypolitics/maryland -funded-african-american-resettlement-colony-in-liberia/.

Gates, Henry Louis. "Who Led the First Back-to-Africa Effort?" *The African Americans: Many Rivers to Cross*. PBS, January 4, 2013. Accessed April 1, 2024. https://www.pbs.org/wnet/african-americans-many-rivers-to-cross/history /who-led-the-1st-back-to-africa-effort/.

Guyatt, Nicholas. "The American Colonization Society: 200 Years of the Colonizing Trick." Black Perspectives. African American Intellectual History Society, December 22, 2016. https://www.aaihs.org/the-american -colonization-society-200-years-of-the-colonizing-trick/.

Magness, Phillip W. "The Île à Vache: From Hope to Disaster." The Opinionator. *New York Times*, April 12, 2013. Accessed April 14, 2024. https://archive.nytimes.com/opinionator.blogs.nytimes.com/2013/04/12 /the-le-vache-from-hope-to-disaster/.

Magness, Phillip W., and Sebastian N. Page. *Colonization After Emancipation: Lincoln and the Movement for Black Resettlement*. Columbia: University of Missouri, 2011.

Mobley, Tianna. "Paul Cuffe & President James Madison: The Trans-Atlantic Emigration Project & the White House." Rubenstein Center Scholarship. The White House Historical Association, September 10, 2021. Accessed April 14, 2024. https://www.whitehousehistory.org/paul-cuffe-president-james-madison -the-transatlantic-emigration-project-the-white-house.

"Pre–Civil War African American Slavery." US History Primary Source Timeline. Library of Congress. Accessed April 14, 2024. https://www.loc.gov /classroom-materials/united-states-history-primary-source-timeline/national -expansion-and-reform-1815-1880/pre-civil-war-african-american-slavery/.

Robinson, Morgan. "The American Colonization Society." Rubenstein Center Scholarship. The White House Historical Association, June 22, 2020. Accessed April 14, 2024. https://www.whitehousehistory.org/the-american-col onization-society.

Sledge, John. Historian/author, *Mobile Bay Magazine*. In discussion with the author. April 2024.

Stevenson, Rhianna. "American Colonization of Liberia." Enduring Connections: Exploring Delmarva's Black History. Edward H. Nabb Research Center for Delmarva History & Culture, June 22, 2022. Accessed April 15, 2024. https:// enduringconnections.salisbury.edu/story/american-colonization-of-liberia.

Vorenberg, Michael. "Abraham Lincoln and the Politics of Black Colonization." *Journal of the Abraham Lincoln Association*, vol. 14, no. 2 (Summer 1993): 22–45. https://quod.lib.umich.edu/j/jala/2629860.0014.204/—abraham-lincoln-and -the-politics-of-black-colonization?rgn=main;view=fulltext.

Waselkov, Gregory A. Professor emeritus of anthropology, Archaeology Department, University of South Alabama. In discussion with the author. April 2024.

Wilde, Ryan Andrew, producer. "Who Was Nance Legins-Costley?" *The 21st Show* (podcast). February 22, 2021. Accessed March 20, 2024. https://will.illinois .edu/21stshow/story/nance-legins-costley.

Chapter 13: The Last Slave Ship: The *Clotilda*

"Act Prohibiting the Importation of Slaves." Southern New Hampshire University, Shapiro Library. October 5, 2021. Accessed March 5, 2024. https://libguides .snhu.edu/c.php?g=1184812&p=8902755#:~:text=The%201807%20Act%20 %20to%20Prohibit,%2C%20Section%209%2C%20Clause%201.

Brown, Margaret, director. *Descendant*. Simi Valley, CA: Higher Ground, 2022. https://www.netflix.com/title/81586731.

Crockett, Norman L. *Black Towns*. Lawrence: University Press of Kansas, 2021.

Diouf, Sylviane A. *Dreams of Africa in Alabama: The Slave Ship Clotilda and the Story of the Last Africans Brought to America*. Northamptonshire, England: Oxford University Press, February 18, 2009.

Jefferson, Thomas. "From Thomas Jefferson to United States Congress, 2 December 1806." *National Archives Founders Online*. Accessed March 5, 2024. https:// founders.archives.gov/documents/Jefferson/99-01-02-4616.

Raines, Ben. *The Last Slave Ship*. New York: Simon & Schuster, 2022.

————. "The Last Slave Ship." Presentation at Alabama Author's Day, Five Rivers Delta Resource Center, Spanish Fort, Alabama, February 20, 2022.

"Voices of the *Clotilda*: Violent Uprooting, Captive Passage, Slavery, and Legacy." The Enterprise Center. Accessed March 5, 2024. https://dignityjustified.com /new-page-1.

Chapter 14: Catfishing Before It Was a Thing: The Story of Flossie Lee

Harris, Aisha. "Who Coined the Term 'Catfish'?" Brow Beat. Slate.com, January 18, 2023. Accessed March 15, 2024. https://slate.com/culture/2013/01/catfish -meaning-and-definition-term-for-online-hoaxes-has-a-surprisingly-long -history.html.

HParkins. "Before Playboy, There Was Flossie." Pieces of History. National Archives, October 20, 2010. Accessed March 15, 2024. https://prologue.blogs.archives .gov/tag/miss-flossie-lee/.

McAnear, Tom. Textual Reference Archives, National Archives at College Park, Maryland. In discussion with the author. April 2024.

Petillo, Brian. "Miss Flossie Lee: The Patron Saint of Simps." *YouTube*, December 18, 2020. Video, 15:53. https://youtu.be/VFsDAnb7MsI. W. L. Bartlett to Art Photograph Co. National Archives Record Group 118: Records of US Attorneys, Series Case Files, Washington, DC. https://catalog.archives.gov /id/183532343.

Chapter 15: When the "Noble Experiment" Turned Deadly

Aaron, Paul, and David Musto. "Temperance and Prohibition in America: A Historical Overview." Alcohol and Public Policy: Beyond the Shadow of Prohibition. National Library of Medicine, 1981. Accessed March 1, 2024. https://www.ncbi .nlm.nih.gov/books/NBK216414/#:~:text=The%20American%20Society%20 of%20Temperance,to%20abstain%20from%20hard%20liquor.

Blum, Deborah. "The Chemist's War: The Little Told Story of How the U.S. Government Poisoned Alcohol during Prohibition with Deadly Consequences." February 19, 2010. Accessed March 2, 2024. https://slate.com/technol ogy/2010/02/the-little-told-story-of-how-the-u-s-government-poisoned-alco hol-during-prohibition.html.

Chen, Angus. "Bad Poetry, Great Booze: The Story of Hidden Bootlegger's Manual." *The Salt*. NPR.org, December 18, 2015. Accessed March 3, 2024. https:// www.npr.org/sections/thesalt/2015/12/18/457411276/bad-poetry-great -booze-the-story-of-the-hidden-bootleggers-manual.

"18th Amendment 1919 (National Prohibition Act). Bureau of Alcohol, Tobacco, and Firearms, September 28, 2016. Accessed March 1, 2024. https://www.atf.gov /our-history/timeline/18th-amendment-1919-national-prohibition-act#:~:text =January%2019%2C%201919%2C%20Congress%20ratified,and%20 transport%20of%20alcoholic%20beverages.

History.com editors. "Prohibition." History.com, April 24, 2023. Accessed March 2, 2024. https://www.history.com/topics/roaring-twenties/prohibition.

Jones, Charles R., Alonzo E. Wilson, and Fred D. L. Squires. *American Prohibition Yearbook 1910.* Chicago: The National Prohibition Press, 1910.

Lerner, Michael. "Unintended Consequences of Prohibition." *Prohibition: A Film by Ken Burns and Lynn Novick.* PBS.ORG, December 6, 2018. https://www.pbs .org/kenburns/prohibition/unintended-consequences.

Lincoln, Abraham. "Abraham Lincoln's Temperance Address of 1842." Speeches and Writings. Abraham Lincoln Online. Accessed March 1, 2024. https://www .abrahamlincolnonline.org/lincoln/speeches/temperance.htm#:~:text=Turn%20 now%2C%20to%20the%20temperance,orphans%20starving%2C%20no%20 widows%20weeping.

Lynch, Jacqueline T. *A Tragic Toast to Christmas: The Infamous Wood Alcohol Deaths of 1919 in Chicopee, Massachusetts.* Chicopee, MA: Jacqueline T. Lynch, 2024.

Morel, Lucas E. "Lincoln Among the Reformers: Tempering the Temperance Movement." *Journal of the Abraham Lincoln Association,* vol. 20, no. 1 (Winter 1999): 1–34. https://quod.lib.umich.edu/j/jala/2629860.0020.103/--lincoln -among-the-reformers-tempering-the-temperance?rgn=main;view=fulltext.

National Museum of American History. "100 Years Later, Do We Think Prohibition Was Good for the Nation?" Smithsonian. Smithsonian Institute, January 17, 2020. Accessed March 1, 2024. https://www.si.edu/object/100-years-lat er-do-we-think-prohibition-was-good-nation%3Aposts_0ddf57dbdbbe 3ba166dc7c9b8ea1d574#:~:text=During%20Prohibition%2C%20denatured%20 ethyl%20alcohol,from%20unregulated%20and%20tainted%20alcohol.

Okrent, Daniel. *Last Call: The Rise and Fall of Prohibition.* New York: Simon & Schuster, 2011.

Prohibition: An Interactive History. "Alcohol as Medicine and Poison." The Mob Museum, November 17, 2016. Accessed March 2, 2024. https://pro hibition.themobmuseum.org/the-history/the-prohibition-underworld /alcohol-as-medicine-and-poison/.

———. "Odd Facts and Stories from Prohibition." The Mob Museum, November 28, 2016. Accessed March 3, 2024. https://prohibition.themobmuseum.org /the-history/prohibition-potpourri/did-you-know/.

Rosen, Dennis. "Poison's Legacy." *Canadian Medical Association Journal,* vol. 182, no. 16 (November 9, 2010): 1767. https://www.cmaj.ca/content/cmaj/182/16/1767 .full.pdf.

"Secrets of Prohibition Era Speakeasies." Ram Cat Cellar Wine & Craft, October 19, 2022. Accessed March 3, 2024. https://www.ramcatcellars.com /secrets-of-prohibition-era-speakeasies/.

Chapter 16: The "First" Female US President

Black, Allida. "Edith Bolling Galt Wilson." First Families. The White House, January 12, 2021. Accessed March 14, 2024. https://www.whitehouse.gov /about-the-white-house/first-families/edith-bolling-galt-wilson/.

Brown, Victoria. "Wilson, Roosevelt, Obama: First Ladies Lead on Food." Viewpoints. John Hopkins Center for a Livable Future, October 9, 2017. Accessed March 14, 2014. https://clf.jhsph.edu/viewpoints/wilson-roosevelt -obama-first-ladies-lead-food.

Dupont Circle. "First Lady Edith Bolling Wilson's Home: 1308 20th St. NW." *YouTube*, February 10, 2022. Video, 21:59. https://www.youtube.com/watch ?v=fKP7vnTE_68.

"Edith Wilson." US Presidents: Woodrow Wilson. University of Virginia Miller Center, August 8, 2023. Accessed March 14, 2024. https://millercenter.org /president/wilson/essays/wilson-edith-1913-firstlady.

"Edith Wilson." The White House Historical Association, June 22, 2020. Accessed April 14, 2024. https://www.whitehousehistory.org/bios/edith-wilson.

Hazelgrove, William. *Madam President: The Secret Presidency of Edith Wilson.* Washington, DC: Regnery History, 2016.

Inskeep, Steve, reporter. "The Sunday Story: America's First Female President?" *Up First Sunday* (podcast), NPR. Accessed March 14, 2024. https://www .npr.org/2023/03/14/1163492487/the-sunday-story-americas-first-female -president.

"Letter from President Woodrow Wilson to His Fiancée, Edith Bolling Galt." Wilson Center. Accessed March 14, 2024. https://www.wilsoncenter.org/sites /default/files/media/documents/page/lovelettertoedith.pdf.

Markel, Howard. "When a Secret President Ran the Country." Health. *PBS NewsHour*, October 2, 2015. Accessed March 14, 2024. https://www.pbs.org /newshour/health/woodrow-wilson-stroke.

Roberts, Rebecca Boggs. *Untold Power: The Fascinating Rise and Complex Legacy of First Lady Edith Wilson.* New York: Penguin Random House, 2023.

Weingroff, Richard F. "On the Road with President Woodrow Wilson." Federal Highway Administration PDF. Accessed April 14, 2024. https://www.fhwa.dot .gov/highwayhistory/wilson.pdf.

Wilson, Edith Bolling. *My Memoir.* New York: Viking–Penguin Random House, 2023.

Chapter 17: Melton Barker, *The Kidnapper's Foil*, and Itinerant Films

Cieslik-Miskimen, Caitlin. "Hollywood in the Hinterland: Newspapers, Itinerant Films and Community Identity in the 1920s." *Communication, Culture and Critique*, vol. 12, no. 3 (September 2019): 378–96, https://doi.org/10.1093 /ccc/tcz016.

Craig, Robert D. "Melton Barker and the Kidnapper's Foil." *Arkansas Historical Society* (May 2011): 14–23. https://www.meltonbarker.org/wp-content/uploads /2012/10/Melton-Barker-Newport-AR-7-6-11.pdf.

"Early Motion Picture Productions." Inventing Entertainment. Library of Congress. Accessed March 15, 2024. https://www.loc.gov/collections/edison -company-motion-pictures-and-sound-recordings/articles-and-essays/history -of-edison-motion-pictures/early-motion-picture-productions/.

Edison, Thomas, and William Heise. "The First Kiss Ever on Film (April 1896): The Rice Irwin Kiss and the Widow Jones," filmed 1896, Internet Archives, 1:08. https://archive.org/details/TheKiss1896.

Frick, Caroline. "Itinerant Filmography, North America." *The Moving Image* 10, no. 1 (2010): 170–81. muse.jhu.edu/article/405405.

———. "Jackrabbit Genius: Melton Barker, Itinerant Films, and Creating Locality." *The Moving Image* 10, no. 1 (2010): 1-22. https://muse.jhu.edu/article/405389.

———. "Hollywood Comes to Town: Preserving Community Films of Cultural Significance in Texas." *Texas Heritage* 1 (Spring 2014): 8–12. Accessed March 1, 2024. https://www.meltonbarker.org/wp-content/uploads/2014/04/Hollywood-Comes-to-Town-Texas-Heritage-Magazine.pdf.

Garcia, Chris. "The Enigmatic Auteur: Part Hal Roach, Part P. T. Barnum." *Austin-American Statesman*. November 26, 2005. Accessed March 2, 2024. https://www.meltonbarker.org/wp-content/uploads/2012/10/the_enigmatic_auteur.pdf.

———. "What Became of Melton Barker." *Austin-American Statesman*. December 30, 2005. Accessed March 2, 2024. https://www.meltonbarker.org/wp-content/uploads/2012/10/what_became_of_melton_barker.pdf.

Hunt, Kristin. "The First Movie Kiss." *JStor Daily*. JStor, May 7, 2020. Accessed March 15, 2024. https://daily.jstor.org/the-first-movie-kiss/.

Pryluck, Calvin. "The Itinerant Movie Show and the Development of the Film Industry." *Journal of the University Film and Video Association* 35, no. 4 (1983): 11–22. http://www.jstor.org/stable/20686967.

Streible, Dan. "Itinerant Filmmakers and Amateur Casts: A Homemade 'Our Gang', 1926." *Film History* 15, no. 2 (2003): 177–92. http://www.jstor.org/stable/3815509.

Chapter 18: The Battle of Los Angeles

Andrews, Evan. "5 Attacks on US Soil During World War II." World War II. *History.com*, August 23, 2023. Accessed March 24, 2024. https://www.history.com/news/5-attacks-on-u-s-soil-during-world-war-ii.

Boissoneault, Lorraine. "The Great Los Angeles Air Raid Terrified Citizens—Even though No Bombs Were Dropped." History of Now. *Smithsonian Magazine*, January 19, 2018. Accessed March 20, 2024. https://www.smithsonianmag.com/history/great-los-angeles-air-raid-terrified-citizenseven-though-no-bombs-were-dropped-180967890/.

"Bombs Fall on Oregon: Japanese Attacks on the State." Life on the Home Front. Oregon Secretary of State. Accessed March 14, 2024. https://sos.oregon.gov/archives/exhibits/ww2/Pages/threats-bombs.aspx#:~:text=On%20June%2020%20%2C%201942%2C%20I,to%20safety%20in%20Neah%20Bay.&text=Casualties%20amounted%20to%20one%20soldier,rushing%20to%20his%20battle%20station.

Charles River Editors. *The Battle of Los Angeles: The History of the Notorious False Alarm That Caused an Artillery Barrage over California during World War II.* Scotts Valley, CA: CreateSpace Independent Publishing Platform, 2018.

Craven, Wesley Frank, and James Lea Cate. "The Army Air Forces in World War II; Defense of the Western Hemisphere." West Coast Air Defenses. The Museum of the City of San Francisco. Accessed March 20, 2024. https://sfmuseum.org/hist9/aaf2.html.

Davies, Lawrence E. "Hails of Los Angeles Air Defense." *New York Times*, February 27, 1942. Accessed March 20, 2024. https://timesmachine.nytimes.com/timesmachine/1942/02/27/85023062.html?pageNumber=3.

———. "Foes Shells Fall on Oregon Coast." *New York Times*, June 23, 1942. Accessed March 20, 2024. https://timesmachine.nytimes.com/timesmachine/1942/06/23/87713224.pdf?pdf_redirect=true&ip=0.

Harrison, Scott. "From the Archives: The 1942 Battle of L.A." *Los Angeles Times*, February 23, 2017. Accessed March 20, 2024. https://www.latimes.com/visuals/framework/la-me-fw-archives-1942-battle-la-20170221-story.html.

Lilley, Kevin. "UFOs or No, Battle of Los Angeles Nears 75th Anniversary." Off Duty. *Military Times*, February 19, 2017. Accessed March 20, 2024. https://www.militarytimes.com/off-duty/2017/02/19/ufos-or-no-battle-of-los-angeles-nears-75th-anniversary/.

Rogers, David J. "How Geologists Unraveled the Mystery of Japanese Vengeance Balloon Bombs in World War II." Missouri University of Science and Technology. Accessed March 20, 2024. https://web.mst.edu/~rogersda/forensic_geology/japenese%20vengenance%20bombs%20new.htm.

Webber, Bert. *Silent Siege III: Japanese Attacks on North America in World War II: Ships Sunk, Air Raids, Bombs Dropped, Civilians Killed*. Princeton, NJ: Webb Research Group, 1992.

Chapter 19: How the "Capricious and Cantankerous" Limping Lady Helped Win World War II

Boyer, Crispin. *Top Secret: Spies, Code, Capers, Gadgets and Classified Cases Revealed*. New York: National Geographic, 2021.

Fausone, James G. "Virginia Hall: An Extraordinary Woman and Exceptional Spy." Home of Heroes, May 3, 2022. Accessed March 5, 2024. https://homeofheroes.com/heroes-stories/world-war-ii/virginia-hall/.

Graham, Brad, and Kathy McGowan. *101 Spy Gadgets for the Evil Genius*. New York: McGraw Hill / Tab Electronics, 2006.

Gralley, Craig. *Hall of Mirrors: Virginia Hall—America's Greatest Spy of World War II*. Chicago: Chrysalis Books, 2019.

Herron, Mick. "The Cool Headed, One-Legged Spy Who Changed the Course of World War II." What to Read. *New York Times*, May 24, 2019. Accessed March 5, 2024. https://www.nytimes.com/2019/05/24/books/review/sonia-purnell-woman-no-importance-virginia-hall.html.

Katz, Brigit. "How a Spy Known as the 'Limping Lady' Helped the Allies Win WWII." Women Who Shaped History. *Smithsonian Magazine*, April 9, 2020. Accessed March 5, 2024. https://www.smithsonianmag.com/history/how-spy-known-limping-lady-helped-allies-win-wwii-180971889/.

Maryland Commission for Women. "Virginia Hall: 1906–1982." Maryland Women's Hall of Fame. Accessed March 5, 2024. https://msa.maryland.gov /msa/educ/exhibits/womenshallfame/html/hall.html.

Mitchell, Don. *The Lady Is a Spy: Virginia Hall, World War II's Most Dangerous Secret Agent.* New York: Scholastic Focus, 2019.

Myer, Greg, reporter. "A Woman of No Importance Finally Gets Her Due." *Morning Edition.* Aired April 18, 2019, on *NPR Morning Edition.* https://www.npr .org/2019/04/18/711356336/a-woman-of-no-importance-finally-gets-her-due.

"1945: Virginia Hall—The Limping Lady, Courageous World War II Resistance Organizer." Barrier Breakers in History. *Intelligence.gov*, April 15, 2019. Accessed March 5, 2024. https://www.intelligence.gov/people/barrier -breakers-in-history/662-1945-virginia-hall/.

"Not Bad for a Girl from Baltimore: The Story of Virginia Hall." US Embassy in Estonia. Accessed March 5, 2024. https://ee.usembassy.gov/wp-content/up loads/sites/207/Not-Bad-for-a-Girl-from-Baltimore.pdf.

Purnell, Sonia. *A Woman of No Importance: The Untold Story of the American Spy Who Helped Win World War II.* New York: Penguin, 2019.

Robinson, Lisa. "Virginia Hall's Critical Role as an American Spy—WBAL TV 11 Baltimore." *YouTube*, November 22, 2015. Video, 4:47. https://youtu.be /S2thDkG_RdI.

Rubin, Linda, and Tony Rubin. "The Allies' Most Dangerous Spy Was a Woman: Virginia Hall—United States Holocaust Memorial Museum." *YouTube*, June 16, 2021. Video, 1:02:33. https://youtu.be/pq0UzaRJ520.

Williams, Rudi. "Virginia Hall, the 'Limping Lady of the ODD,' Receives the Distinguished Service Cross, the Nation's Second Highest Award for Valor in Combat. She Was the Only Civilian Woman to Receive the Award During World War II." 1945. JPG. 0.03MB. US Department of Defense, Washington, https://www.defense.gov/Multimedia/Photos/igphoto/2001088184/.

Chapter 20: A Femme Fatale, a Poison Pen, and a Killer Milkshake

Anderson, Jack, and Whitten, Les. "CIA Plots Against Castro Recounted." *Washington Post*, March 10, 1975. Accessed March 1, 2024. https://www.cia. gov/readingroom/docs/CIA-RDP88-01315R000300510158-2.pdf.

CIA. *Intelligence Report on CIA Assassination Plots (1).* June 5, 1975. Accessed March 1, 2024. https://www.fordlibrarymuseum.gov/library/document/0005 /7324009.pdf.

Escalante, Fabian. *634 Ways to Kill Fidel.* New York: Seven Stories Press, 2021.

Kratz, Jessie. "Fidel Castro's Childhood Plea to President Roosevelt." Pieces of History. National Archives, September 26, 2014. Accessed March 1, 2024. https://pro logue.blogs.archives.gov/2010/11/16/the-must-have-christmas-gift-of-1864/.

Lorenz, Martia. *Marita: The Spy Who Loved Castro: A Memoir by Marita Lorenz.* New York: Pegasus Books, 2017.

Matthews, Dylan. "7 Bizarre Ways the U.S. Tried to Kill or Topple Fidel Castro." VOX.com., November 26, 2016. Accessed March 1, 2024. https://www.vox .com/2016/11/26/13752514/us-fidel-castro-assassination.

Reuters. "Closest CIA Bid to Kill Castro Was Poisoned Drink." *Reuters*, August 9, 2007. Accessed March 10, 2024. https://www.reuters.com/article/idUSN 04279351/.

US Senate Select Committee to Study Governmental Operations with Respect to Intelligence Activities. *Alleged Assassination Plots Involving Foreign Leaders: 1975 Report on CIA Covert Operations to Kill Fidel Castro, Ngo Dinh Dehm, and Others*. 1975. Accessed March 1, 2024. https://www.aarclibrary.org/publib/church/re ports/ir/pdf/ChurchIR_3B_Cuba.pdf.

Warren, Raymond A., acting chief, Latin American Division. *Documentation of Castro Assassination Plots*. August 11, 1975. Accessed March 1, 2024. https:// www.archives.gov/files/research/jfk/releases/2022/104-10103-10183.pdf.

Chapter 21: Come Fly with Me . . . to the Moon

Arthur, Charles. "USSR Planned to Atom Bomb the Moon," *Independent*, July 9, 1999. Accessed March 1, 2024. https://www.independent.co.uk/news/ussr -planned-to-atom-bomb-moon-1105344.html.

"Card, Club, Pan Am, 'First Moon Flights'". Collection Objects. National Air and Space Museum, Accessed March 15, 2024. https://airandspace.si.edu/col lection-objects/card-club-pan-am-first-moon-flights/nasm_A20180010000.

Chertok, Boris. *Rockets and People: Hot Days of the Cold War Vol. III*. Washington, DC: US Government Printing Office, 2009. https://www.nasa.gov/wp-content/up loads/2015/04/636007main_RocketsPeopleVolume3-ebook.pdf?emrc=03734e.

Hilton, Conrad. *Be My Guest*. New York: Simon & Schuster, 1994.

Leadbeater, Chris. "The Strange Story of the Hilton Hotel on the Moon, and the Serious Plan to Build It." Travel/Destinations. *The Telegraph*, July 18, 2019. Accessed March 15, 2024. https://www.telegraph.co.uk/travel/destinations /north-america/united-states/articles/strange-tale-Hilton-lunar-hotel-moon/.

Lengeman, William, III. "Space Tourism's First Small Steps." *Air and Space Magazine*. Smithsonian Institute, September 2007. Accessed March 10, 2024. https://www.smithsonianmag.com/air-space-magazine/space-tourisms-first -small-steps-20428780/.

Mayer, Daisy von Scherler, director. *Mad Men*. Season 3, episode 7, "Seven Twenty Three." Written by Matthew Weiner, Andre Jacquemetton, Maria Jacquemetton. Aired September 27, 2009, on AMC. https://www.imdb.com/title/tt1472778 /https://www.imdb.com/title/tt1472778/.

Stamler, Hannah. "Long Before SpaceX, Pan Am was Booking Flights to the Moon." *Humanities*, vol. 43, no. 4 (Fall 2022), National Endowment for the Humanities. Accessed March 15, 2024. https://www.neh.gov/article/long -spacex-pan-am-was-booking-flights-moon.

About the Author

Joe Cuhaj grew up in northern New Jersey, where his love of discovering obscure and offbeat tales of history was nurtured by his history-loving family and exceptional high school history teachers. The former radio broadcaster now lives in L.A. (Lower Alabama) on the Gulf Coast and is the author of nineteen books, thirteen of which are outdoor recreation guides published by FalconGuides and Menasha Ridge Press on hiking, kayaking, and camping in the Southeast and along the Gulf Coast. He has also written six nonfiction history books, including Prometheus Books titles *Space Oddities: Forgotten Stories of Mankind's Exploration of Space* and *Everyone's Gone to the Moon: July 1969, Life on Earth, and the Epic Voyage of Apollo 11.*